D1335067

The Confidential Clerk

By T. S. Eliot

THE COMPLETE POEMS AND PLAYS OF T. S. ELIOT

verse
COLLECTED POEMS 1909–1962
FOUR QUARTETS
THE WASTE LAND *and* OTHER POEMS
THE WASTE LAND
A facsimile and transcript of the original drafts
Edited by Valerie Eliot
INVENTIONS OF THE MARCH HARE:
Poems 1909–1917 Edited by Christopher Ricks
SELECTED POEMS
OLD POSSUM'S BOOK OF PRACTICAL CATS

correspondence
THE LETTERS OF T. S. ELIOT
Volume 1 – 1898–1922
Edited by Valerie Eliot

plays
MURDER IN THE CATHEDRAL
THE FAMILY REUNION
THE COCKTAIL PARTY
THE CONFIDENTIAL CLERK
THE ELDER STATESMAN

literary criticism
SELECTED ESSAYS
THE USE OF POETRY *and* THE USE OF CRITICISM
TO CRITICIZE THE CRITIC
ON POETRY AND POETS
THE VARIETIES OF METAPHYSICAL POETRY
Edited by Ronald Schuchard
SELECTED PROSE OF T. S. ELIOT
Edited by Frank Kermode

social criticism
THE IDEA OF A CHRISTIAN SOCIETY
Edited by David Edwards
NOTES TOWARDS THE DEFINITION OF CULTURE

THE
CONFIDENTIAL CLERK
A PLAY
by
T. S. ELIOT

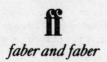

faber and faber

First published in 1954
by Faber and Faber Limited
3 Queen Square London WC1N 3AU
Reprinted 1974, 1979 and 1991

Printed and bound in Great Britain by
Mackays of Chatham PLC, Chatham, Kent

ISBN 0–571–08162–2

6 8 10 9 7 5

THE evolution of this play from the earliest draft to the final text, has been influenced at every stage by suggestions offered, and by objections raised, by Mr. E. Martin Browne and Mr. John Hayward, to both of whom I wish to make grateful acknowledgment.

T. S. E.

November 1953

Characters

SIR CLAUDE MULHAMMER
EGGERSON
COLBY SIMPKINS
B. KAGHAN
LUCASTA ANGEL
LADY ELIZABETH MULHAMMER
MRS. GUZZARD

Act One

The Business Room on the first floor of SIR CLAUDE
MULHAMMER'S *London house. Early afternoon.* SIR
CLAUDE *writing at desk. Enter* EGGERSON.

SIR CLAUDE

Ah, there you are, Eggerson! Punctual as always.
I'm sorry to have to bring you up to London
All the way from Joshua Park, on an errand like this.
But you know my wife wouldn't like anyone to meet her
At Northolt, but you. And I couldn't send Colby.
That's not the way to arrange their first meeting,
On her return from Switzerland.

EGGERSON

Impossible, Sir Claude!
A very delicate situation —
Her first meeting with Mr. Simpkins.
But I was glad of the excuse for coming up to London:
I've spent the morning shopping! Gardening tools.
The number of things one needs for a garden!
And I thought, now's the moment to buy some new tools
So as not to lose a moment at the end of the winter.
And I matched some material for Mrs. E.,
Which she's been wanting. So *she*'ll be pleased.
Then I lunched at the store — they have a restaurant;
An excellent lunch, and cheap, for nowadays.
But where's Mr. Simpkins? Will he be here?

SIR CLAUDE

I had to send him to the City this morning,
But he'll be back, I hope, before you leave.

EGGERSON

And how's he getting on? Swimmingly, I'm sure,
As I've heard nothing since the last time I came.

SIR CLAUDE

Well, of course, Eggerson, you're irreplaceable . . .

EGGERSON

Oh, Sir Claude, you shouldn't say that!
Mr. Simpkins is far better qualified than I was
To be your confidential clerk.
He was finding his feet, very quickly,
During the time we worked together.
All he needs is confidence.

SIR CLAUDE

And experience.
With a young man, some readjustment is necessary.
But I'm satisfied that he's getting the hang of things,
And I think he's beginning to take a keen interest.

EGGERSON

And getting over his disappointment?
Of course, I never mentioned that:
It's only what you told me.

SIR CLAUDE

About his music.
Yes, I think so. I understand his feelings.
He's like me, Eggerson. The same disappointment
In a different form. He won't forget
That his great ambition was to be an organist,
Just as I can't forget . . . no matter.
The great thing was to find something else
He could do, and do well. And I think he's found it,
Just as I did. I shall tell him about myself.
But so far, I've left him to his own devices:
I thought he would fall into this way of life more quickly
If we started on a purely business basis.

EGGERSON

No doubt that's best. While he's still living
With his aunt in Teddington, and coming up daily
Just as I used to. And the flat in the mews?
How soon will that be ready for him?

SIR CLAUDE

They have still to do the walls. And then it must be furnished.
I'm trying to find him a really good piano.

EGGERSON

A piano? Yes, I'm sure he'll feel at home
When he has a piano. You think of everything.
But if I might make a suggestion: window boxes!
He's expressed such an interest in my garden
That I think he ought to have window boxes.
Some day, he'll want a garden of his own. And yes, a bird
     bath!

SIR CLAUDE

A bird bath? In the mews? What's the point of that?

EGGERSON

He told me he was very fond of bird watching.

SIR CLAUDE

But there won't be any birds — none worth watching.

EGGERSON

I don't know, Sir Claude. Only the other day
I read a letter in *The Times* about wild birds seen in London:
And I'm sure Mr. Simpkins will find them, if anybody.

SIR CLAUDE

Well, we'll leave that for the present. As we have a little
     time
Before you start for Northolt — the car will be ready —
Let's think what you're to say to Lady Elizabeth,

9

Coming back from the airport, about Colby.
I think, you ought to give her warning
Of whom she is to meet on her arrival.

EGGERSON

How would you like me to approach the subject?

SIR CLAUDE

Of course, she knows you were wanting to retire,
As we had some discussion about replacing you.
But you know she regards you — well, completely
As one of the household.

EGGERSON

          That's a great compliment.

SIR CLAUDE

And well deserved; but rather inconvenient
When it comes to appointing a successor.
Makes it very difficult to replace you.
She thinks she ought to have a hand in the choosing;
And besides, she is convinced that she, of all people,
Is a better judge of character than I am.

EGGERSON

Oh, I wouldn't say that, Sir Claude!
She has too much respect for your business genius.
But it's true she believes she has what she calls 'guidance'.

SIR CLAUDE

Guidance. That's worse than believing in her judgment:
We could argue about that. You can't argue with guidance.
But if she appears to be puzzled, or annoyed
At my making the appointment during her absence,
You must say you had to leave under medical orders.
She's always been concerned about your state of health,
So she'll be sympathetic. And as for Colby —
Say that Mr. Simpkins was highly recommended,

And say that I had to make a quick decision
Because he'd had another very tempting offer.
Something like that. Don't make too much of it.
And I rather hope that she will take to him at once:
If so, she is certain to come to believe
That she chose him herself. By the way, don't forget
To let her know that he's very musical.
She can take him to concerts. But don't overdo it!

EGGERSON
I'll remember that. Music.

SIR CLAUDE
                              And by the way,
How much have you actually told him about her?
You remember, I asked you to prepare him a little;
There are some things you could say better than I could,
And ways in which you could reassure him
Better than I. He's more at ease with you
Than he is with me.

EGGERSON
                              Oh, you mustn't say that!
Though I've done my best to gain his confidence.
I did mention her interest in Light from the East.

SIR CLAUDE
And the Book of Revelation? And the Wisdom of Atlantis?

EGGERSON
Well, to tell the truth, Sir Claude, I only touched on these
        matters,
They're much too deep for me. And I thought, Mr. Simpkins,
He's highly educated. He'll soon begin to grasp them.
No, I haven't told him much about Lady Elizabeth.
But there's one thing I should like to know —
If you don't mind — before I go to meet her.
How soon do you propose to . . . *explain* Mr. Simpkins?

Regularize his position in the household?
You told me that was your eventual intention.

SIR CLAUDE

When — or indeed whether — I reveal his identity
Depends on how she takes to him. This afternoon
She will only learn that you have finally retired
And that you have a young successor,
A Mr. Colby Simpkins.

EGGERSON
Merely Mr. Simpkins.

SIR CLAUDE

The reasons for starting him during her absence
Are perfectly clear. But beyond that point
I haven't yet explained my plans to you.
Why I've never told her about him,
The reason for meeting him as merely Mr. Simpkins,
Is, that she has a strong maternal instinct . . .

EGGERSON

I realise that.

SIR CLAUDE
Which has always been thwarted.

EGGERSON

I'm sure it's been a grief to both of you
That you've never had children.

SIR CLAUDE

No worse, Eggerson,
Than for you and your wife, to have had a son
Lost in action, and his grave unknown.

EGGERSON

And you're thinking no doubt that Lady Elizabeth
Would be put in mind of the child *she* lost.

SIR CLAUDE

In a very different way, yes. You might say *mislaid*,
Since the father is dead, and there's no way of tracing it.
Yes, I was thinking of her missing child:
In the circumstances, that might make her jealous.
I've explained all this to Colby — Mr. Simpkins.

EGGERSON

I see what you mean.

SIR CLAUDE

She must get to like him first:
And then, Eggerson, I am not unhopeful
That, under the impression that he is an orphan,
She will want us to adopt him.

EGGERSON

Adopt him! Yes, indeed,
That would be the solution. Yes, quite ideal.

SIR CLAUDE

I'm glad you agree. Your support will be helpful.

EGGERSON

I'm sure I shall be very happy to commend him.

SIR CLAUDE

You mustn't overdo it! But your approval matters.
You know she thinks the world of your opinion.

EGGERSON

Well, I believe that once or twice, perhaps . . .
But I'm afraid you overrate my influence.
I have never been able to make her like Miss Angel;
She becomes abstracted, whenever I mention her.

SIR CLAUDE

But she knew about Lucasta — Miss Angel, from the start.
That was one difficulty. And there are others.
For one, they're both of them women.

EGGERSON

True.

SIR CLAUDE

But I don't think she takes much notice of Miss Angel.
She doesn't see her. And Miss Angel
Will soon be getting married, I expect.

EGGERSON

And so I hope. A most suitable arrangement.
But will you tell me this: if it comes to the point
At which Lady Elizabeth wants to adopt him —
An admirable solution — then what follows?
Will you let her know, then, that Mr. Simpkins
Is actually your son?

SIR CLAUDE

That's where I'm in the dark.
I simply can't guess what her reaction would be.
There's a lot I don't understand about my wife.
There's always something one's ignorant of
About anyone, however well one knows them;
And that may be something of the greatest importance.
It's when you're sure you understand a person
That you're liable to make the worst mistake about him.
As a matter of fact, there's a lot I don't know
About you, Eggerson, although we worked together
For nearly thirty years.

EGGERSON

Nearly thirty-one.
But now you put it so convincingly,
I must admit there's a lot that *I* don't understand
About my wife.

SIR CLAUDE

And just as much
She just doesn't know about you. And just as much

14

You don't know about me — I'm not so sure of that!
My rule is to remember that I understand nobody,
But on the other hand never to be sure
That they don't understand me — a good deal better
Than I should care to think, perhaps.

EGGERSON

           And do I infer
That you're not sure you understand Mr. Simpkins, either?

SIR CLAUDE

A timely reminder. You may have to repeat it.
But he should be back by now. And then I'll leave you.
I must telephone to Amsterdam, and possibly to Paris.
But when you return with Lady Elizabeth
I'll be ready waiting to introduce him.
[*Enter* COLBY SIMPKINS *with brief case*]

SIR CLAUDE

Ah, Colby, I was just saying to Eggerson
It was time you were back. Was your morning satisfactory?

COLBY

I've got what you wanted, Sir Claude. Good afternoon,
Mr. Eggerson. I was afraid I'd miss you.

EGGERSON

I'm off in half an hour, Mr. Simpkins.

SIR CLAUDE

I'll leave you now. But when Eggerson comes back
With Lady Elizabeth, I will rejoin you.

                [*Exit* SIR CLAUDE]

COLBY

I'm glad you don't have to leave just yet.
I'm rather nervous about this meeting.
You've told me very little about Lady Elizabeth,

And Sir Claude himself hasn't told me very much:
So I've no idea how I ought to behave.
B. Kaghan has told me something about her,
But that's rather alarming.

EGGERSON

        Mr. Kaghan is prejudiced.
He's never hit it off with Lady Elizabeth.
Don't listen to him. He understands Sir Claude,
And he's always been very grateful to Sir Claude,
As he ought to be. Sir Claude picked him out
And gave him his start. And he's made the most of it —
That I will say. An encouraging example
For you, Mr. Simpkins. He'll be a power in the City!
And he has a heart of gold. But not to beat about the bush,
He's rather a rough diamond. Very free and easy ways;
And Lady Elizabeth has never taken to him.
But you, Mr. Simpkins, that's very different.

COLBY

I don't know why it should be so different.
I like B. Kaghan. I've found him very helpful
And very good company apart from business.

EGGERSON

Oh yes, Mr. Kaghan is very good company.
He makes me laugh sometimes. I don't laugh easily.
Quite a humorist, he is. In fact, Mrs. E.
Sometimes says to me: 'Eggerson, why can't you make me laugh
     laugh
The way B. Kaghan did?' She's only met him once;
But do you know, he began addressing her as Muriel —
Within the first ten minutes! I was horrified.
But she actually liked it. Muriel *is* her name.
He has a way with the ladies, you know.
But with Lady Elizabeth he wasn't so successful.
She once referred to him as 'undistinguished';
But with you, as I said, it will be very different.

16

She'll see at once that you're a man of culture;
And besides, she's very musical.

COLBY

Thank you for the warning!

EGGERSON

So if you don't mind, I shall mention at once
That you are a musician.

COLBY

I'll be on my guard.

EGGERSON

Your music will certainly be a great asset
With Lady Elizabeth. I envy you that.
I've always sung in our voluntary choir
And at the carol service. But I wish I was musical.

COLBY

I still don't feel very well prepared for meeting her.
[*A loud knock. Enter* B. KAGHAN]

KAGHAN

Enter B. Kaghan. Hello Colby!
And hello Eggers! I'm glad to find you here.
It's lucky for Colby.

EGGERSON

How so Mr. Kaghan?

KAGHAN

Because Lucasta's with me! The usual catastrophe.
She's come to pry some cash from the money-box.
Bankrupt again! So I thought I'd better bring her
And come upstairs ahead, to ease the shock for Colby.
But as you're here, Eggers, I can just relax.
I'm going to enjoy the game from the sidelines.
[*Enter* LUCASTA ANGEL]

17

LUCASTA

Eggy, I've lost my job!

EGGERSON
Again, Miss Angel?

LUCASTA
Yes, again! And serve them right!

EGGERSON
You have been, I presume, persistently unpunctual.

LUCASTA
You're wrong, Eggy. It's rank injustice.
Two months I'd gone on filing those papers
Which no one ever wanted — at least, not till yesterday.
Then, just by bad luck, the boss did want a letter
And I couldn't find it. And then he got suspicious
And asked for things I'm sure he didn't want —
Just to make trouble! And I couldn't find one of them.
But they're all filed somewhere, I'm sure, so why bother?
But who's this, Eggy? Is it Colby Simpkins?
Introduce him, one or the other of you.

EGGERSON
Mr. Simpkins, Miss Angel. As you know, Miss Angel,
Mr. Simpkins has taken over my duties.

LUCASTA
And does he know that *I*'m one of his duties?
Have you prepared him for taking *me* over?
Did you know that, Colby? I'm Lucasta.
It's only Eggy calls me Miss Angel,
Just to annoy me. Don't you agree
That Lucasta suits me better?

COLBY
I'm sure they both suit you.

18

LUCASTA

Snubbed again! I suppose I asked for it.
That's what comes of being cursed with a name like Angel.
I'm thinking of changing it. But, Colby,
Do you know that I'm one of your responsibilities?

COLBY

No, I'm afraid I didn't know that.

EGGERSON

You mustn't give way to her, Mr. Simpkins.
I never do. I always say
That if you give Miss Angel an inch
She'll take an ell.

LUCASTA

      L. for Lucasta.
Go on, Eggy. Don't mind him, Colby.
Colby, are you married?

COLBY

      No, I'm not married.

LUCASTA

Then I don't mind being seen with you in public.
You may take me out to dinner. A working girl like me
Is often very hungry — living on a pittance —
Cooking a sausage on a gas ring . . .

EGGERSON

You mustn't believe a word she says.

LUCASTA

Mr. Simpkins is going to believe all I say,
Mr. Eggerson. And I know he'll be nice to me
When you're out of the way. Why don't you let him speak?
Eggy's really quite human, Colby.
It's only that he's terrified of Mrs. Eggerson;
That's why he's never asked me out to lunch.

EGGERSON

We will leave Mrs. Eggerson out of this, Miss Angel.

LUCASTA

That's what he always says, Colby,
When I mention Mrs. Eggerson. He never fails to rise.
B.! What have you told Colby about me?

KAGHAN

It's no use telling anybody about you:
Nobody'd ever believe in your existence
Until they met you. Colby's still reeling.
It's going to be my responsibility,
As your fiancé, to protect Colby from you.
But first, let's cope with the financial crisis.

LUCASTA

Yes, Eggy, will you break the sad news to Claude?
Meanwhile, you'll have to raid the till for me. I'm starving.

KAGHAN

I've just given her lunch. The problem with Lucasta
Is how to keep her fed between meals.

LUCASTA

B., you're a beast. I've a very small appetite.
But the point is, that I'm penniless.

KAGHAN

She's had a week's salary is lieu of notice.

LUCASTA

B., remember you're only my fiancé on approval.
Can I have some money, Eggy?

EGGERSON

                    I'm no longer in charge,
And that duty has *not* devolved on Mr. Simpkins:

20

Sir Claude intends to deal with these matters himself.
You will have to ask Sir Claude. But I'll speak to him
When I return from Northolt.

LUCASTA

You're going to meet Lizzie?

EGGERSON

I am meeting Lady Elizabeth at Northolt.

LUCASTA

Well, I don't propose to be on the scene when *she* comes.

KAGHAN

And I don't propose to leave you with Colby.
He's had enough for one day. Take my advice, Colby.
Never allow Lucasta the slightest advantage
Or she'll exploit it. You have to be tough with her;
She's hard as nails. Now I'll take her off your hands.
I'll show you how it's done. Come along, Lucasta,
I'm going to make a day of it, and take you out to tea.

LUCASTA

I'm dying for my tea. The strain of this crisis
Has been too much for me. Another time, Colby.
I'll ring you up, and let you take me out to lunch.

[*Exit* LUCASTA]

KAGHAN

Take it easy, Colby. You'll get used to her.

[*Exit* KAGHAN]

COLBY

Egg . . . Mr. Eggerson!

EGGERSON

Yes, Mr. Simpkins?

COLBY

You seem to me sane. And I think I am.

21

EGGERSON

I have no doubt on either point, none at all.

COLBY

And B. Kaghan has always seemed to me sane.

EGGERSON

I should call him the very picture of sanity.

COLBY

But you never warned me about Miss Angel.
What about *her*?

EGGERSON

Oh, Miss Angel.
She's rather flighty. But she has a good heart.

COLBY

But does she address Sir Claude Mulhammer
As Claude? To his face?

EGGERSON

She does indeed.

COLBY

And does she call Lady Elizabeth *Lizzie*?

EGGERSON

Well, not in her presence. Not when I've been there.
No, I don't think she would. But she does call her Lizzie,
Sometimes, to Sir Claude. And do you know —
I think it amuses him.

COLBY

Well, perhaps I'll be amused.
But it did make my head spin — all those first names
The first time I met her. I'm not used to it.

EGGERSON

You'll soon get used to it. You'll be calling me Eggers
Before you know it!

COLBY

                    I shouldn't wonder.
I nearly did, a moment ago.
Then I'd have been certain I'd lost my reason:
Her influence is perfectly frightening.
But tell me about Lu . . . Miss Angel:
What's her connection with this household?

EGGERSON

Well. A kind of fiduciary relationship.
No, I don't think that's quite the right term.
She's no money of her own, as you may have gathered;
But I think her father was a friend of Sir Claude's,
And he's made himself responsible for her.
In any case, he's behaved like a father —
A very generous man, is Sir Claude.
To tell the truth, she's something of a thorn in his flesh,
Always losing her jobs, because she won't stick to them.
He gives her an allowance — very adequate indeed,
Though she's always in debt. But you needn't worry
About her, Mr. Simpkins. She'll marry Mr. Kaghan
In the end. He's a man who gets his own way,
And I think he can manage her. If anyone can.

COLBY

But is she likely to be a nuisance?

EGGERSON

Not unless you give her encouragement.
I have never encouraged her.

COLBY

                    But you have Mrs. Eggerson.

23

EGGERSON

Yes, she's a great protection. And I have my garden
To protect me against Mrs. E. That's my joke.

COLBY

Well, I've never met anyone like Miss Angel.

EGGERSON

You'll get used to her, Mr. Simpkins.
Time works wonders, that's what I always say.
But I don't expect you'll have to see much of her:
That responsibility's not on your shoulders.
Lady Elizabeth, now, that's different.

COLBY

At least, I don't suppose Lady Elizabeth
Can be quite so unusual as Miss Angel.

EGGERSON

O yes, Mr. Simpkins, much more unusual.

COLBY

Oh!

EGGERSON

Well, as I told you, she really is a lady,
Rather a *grande dame*, as the French say.
That's what Sir Claude admires about her.
He said to me once, in a moment of confidence —
He'd just come back from a public luncheon —
'Eggerson', he said, 'I wanted a lady,
And I'm perfectly satisfied with the bargain.'
Of course it's true that her family connections
Have sometimes been useful. But he didn't think of that:
He's not petty-minded — though nothing escapes him.
And such a generous heart! He's rather a Socialist.
I'm staunch Conservative, myself.

COLBY

But is Lady Elizabeth very unusual
In any other way, besides being a lady?

EGGERSON

Why, yes, indeed, I must admit she is.
Most of her oddities are perfectly harmless.
You'll soon get used to them. That's what Sir Claude said:
'Humour her, Eggerson,' he said, 'humour her.'
But she has one trait that I think I did touch on:
She's very absent-minded.

COLBY

                         I hope you don't mean,
She has lapses of memory?

EGGERSON

                         I didn't mean that.
No. She hasn't very much memory to lose,
Though she sometimes remembers when you least expect it.
But she does forget things. And she likes to travel,
Mostly for her health. And when she's abroad
She is apt to buy a house. And then goes away
And forgets all about it. That can be complicated
And very costly. I've had some rare adventures!
I remember long ago, saying to Mrs. E.,
When we'd bought our house in Joshua Park
(On a mortgage, of course) 'now we've settled down
All the travel *I* want is up to the City
And back to Joshua Park in the evening,
And once a year our holiday at Dawlish'.
And to think that was only the beginning of my travels!
It's been a very unusual privilege
To see as much of Europe as I have,
Getting Lady Elizabeth out of her difficulties.

COLBY

Perhaps she won't even arrive by this plane.

EGGERSON

Oh, that could happen. She sometimes gets lost,
Or loses her ticket, or even her passport.
But let's not be crossing any bridges
Until we come to them. That's what *I* always say.
And I'm sure you'll like her. She's *such* a lady!
And what's more, she has a good heart.

COLBY

Everybody seems to be kind-hearted.
But there's one thing I do believe, Mr. Eggerson:
That *you* have a kind heart. And I'm convinced
That you always contrive to think the best of everyone.

EGGERSON

You'll come to find that I'm right, I assure you.
[*Enter* SIR CLAUDE]

SIR CLAUDE

Hello! Still here? It's time you were off.

EGGERSON

I'm just going. There's plenty of time.
                            [*Looks at his watch*]
I'll arrive at the airport with minutes to spare,
And besides, there's the Customs. That'll take her a time,
From my experience.

LADY ELIZABETH MULHAMMER'S *voice off**

Just open that case, I want something out of it.
Unwrap that — It's a bottle of medicine.
Now, Parkman, will you give it to the driver?
He tells me that he suffers from chronic catarrh.

SIR CLAUDE

Hello! What's that?

* Lady Elizabeth's words off stage are not intended to be heard
distinctly by an audience in the theatre.

[*Opens door on to landing and listens*]
She's here, Eggerson! That's her voice.
Where is she? Oh, she's gone out again.
[*Goes to the window and looks down on the street*]
She's having a conversation with the cabman.
What can they be talking about? She's coming in!

LADY ELIZABETH MULHAMMER'S *voice off**

No, Gertrude, I haven't had any lunch,
And I don't want it now. Just bring me some tea.
Nothing with it. No, I forgot:
You haven't learned yet how to make tea properly.
A cup of black coffee. Is Sir Claude at home?
I'll speak to him first.

SIR CLAUDE

Good heavens, Eggerson, what *can* have happened?

EGGERSON

It's perfectly amazing. Let *me* go down to meet her.

SIR CLAUDE

Where ought we to be? What ought we to be doing?

EGGERSON
[*at the open door*]
She's speaking to the parlourmaid. She's coming up.

SIR CLAUDE

Colby, sit at the desk, and pick up some papers.
We must look as if we'd been engaged in business.
[*Enter* LADY ELIZABETH MULHAMMER]

EGGERSON & SIR CLAUDE
[*simultaneously*]
Lady Elizabeth!
Elizabeth!

* Lady Elizabeth's words off stage are not intended to be heard
distinctly by an audience in the theatre.

SIR CLAUDE

What on earth has happened?

EGGERSON

Lady Elizabeth! This is most surprising.

LADY ELIZABETH

What's surprising, Eggerson? I've arrived, that's all.

EGGERSON

I was just starting for Northolt to meet you.

LADY ELIZABETH

That was very thoughtful of you, Eggerson,
But quite unnecessary. And besides,
I didn't come by air. I arrived at Victoria.

SIR CLAUDE

Do you mean to say that you changed your ticket?

EGGERSON

Yes, how did you manage to change your ticket?

LADY ELIZABETH

I went to the agency and got them to change it.
I can't understand why you're both so surprised.
You know I'm a very experienced traveller.

SIR CLAUDE

Oh yes, of course we know that, Elizabeth.
But why did you change your plans?

LADY ELIZABETH

Because of Mildred
Deverell.
She's been having the treatment with me,
And she can't go by air — she says it makes her sea-sick;
So we took the night train, and did the Channel crossing.
But who is this young man? His face is familiar.

SIR CLAUDE

This young man is Eggerson's successor.
You know that Eggerson's been meaning to retire . . .

EGGERSON

Under medical orders, Lady Elizabeth:
The doctor made it very imperative . . .

SIR CLAUDE

Mr. Simpkins had very strong recommendations . . .

EGGERSON

And at the same time, he had another tempting offer:
So we had to make a quick decision.

SIR CLAUDE

I didn't want to bother you, during your treatment . . .

EGGERSON

And Mr. Simpkins is much more highly qualified
Than I am, to be a confidential clerk.
Besides, he's very musical.

LADY ELIZABETH

Musical?
Isn't this the young man I interviewed
And recommended to Sir Claude? Of course it is.
I remember saying: 'He has a good aura.'
I remember people's auras almost better than their faces.
What did you say his name was?

SIR CLAUDE

Colby Simpkins.

LADY ELIZABETH

[*counting on her fingers*]

Thirteen letters. That's very auspicious —
Contrary to what most people think.

You should be artistic. But you look rather frail.
I must give you lessons in the art of health.
Where is your home, Mr. Colby?

COLBY
Simpkins.

EGGERSON
Mr. Colby Simpkins.

LADY ELIZABETH
I prefer Colby.
Where are you living?

SIR CLAUDE
His home's outside London.
But I want to have him closer at hand —
You know what a bother it's been for Eggerson —
So I'm having the flat in the mews done over.

LADY ELIZABETH
But all in the wrong colours, I'm sure. My husband
Does not understand the importance of colour
For our spiritual life, Mr. Colby.
Neither, I regret to say, does Eggerson.
What colour have you chosen, between you?

SIR CLAUDE
I thought a primrose yellow would be cheerful.

LADY ELIZABETH
Just what I expected. A primrose yellow
Would be absolutely baneful to Mr. Colby.
He needs a light mauve. I shall see about that.
But not today. I shall go and rest now.
In a sleeping-car it is quite impossible
To get one's quiet hour. A quiet hour a day
Is most essential, Dr. Rebmann says.

SIR CLAUDE

Rebmann? I thought it was a Dr. Leroux.

LADY ELIZABETH

Dr. Leroux is in Lausanne.
I have been in Zurich, under Dr. Rebmann.

SIR CLAUDE

But you were going out to Dr. Leroux
In Lausanne. What made you go to Zurich?

LADY ELIZABETH

Why, I'd no sooner got to Lausanne
Than whom should I meet but Mildred Deverell.
She was going on to Zurich. So she said: 'Come to Zurich!
There's a wonderful doctor who teaches mind control.'
So on I went to Zurich.

SIR CLAUDE

                So on you went to Zurich.
But I thought that the doctor in Lausanne taught mind
    control?

LADY ELIZABETH

No, Claude, he only teaches *thought* control.
Mind control is a different matter:
It's more advanced. But I wrote you all about it.

SIR CLAUDE

It's true, you did send me postcards from Zurich;
But you know that I can't decipher your writing.
I like to have the cards, just to know where you are
By reading the postmark.

LADY ELIZABETH

              But Claude, I'm glad to find
That you've taken my advice.

SIR CLAUDE
Your advice? About what?

LADY ELIZABETH
To engage Mr. Colby. I really am distressed!
This is not the first sign that I've noticed
Of your memory failing. I must persuade you
To have a course of treatment with Dr. Rebmann —
No, at your stage, I think, with Dr. Leroux.
Don't you remember, I said before I left:
'Trust my guidance for once, and engage that young man?'
Well, that was Mr. Colby.

SIR CLAUDE
Oh, I see.
Yes, now I am beginning to remember.
I must have acted on your guidance.

LADY ELIZABETH
I must explain to you, Mr. Colby,
That I am to share you with my husband.
You shall have tea with me tomorrow,
And then I shall tell you about my committees.
I must go and rest now.

SIR CLAUDE
Yes, you go and rest.
I'm in the middle of some business with Mr. . . . .

LADY ELIZABETH
Colby!
[*Exit* LADY ELIZABETH]

SIR CLAUDE
She actually went and changed her own ticket.
It's something unheard of.

EGGERSON
Amazing, isn't it!

SIR CLAUDE

If this is what the doctor in Zurich has done for her,
I give him full marks. Well, Eggerson,
I seem to have brought you up to London for nothing.

EGGERSON

Oh, not for nothing! I wouldn't have missed it.
And besides, as I told you, I've done some shopping.
But I'd better be off now. Mr. Simpkins —
If anything *should* turn up unexpected
And you find yourself non-plussed, you must get me on the
    phone.
If I'm not in the house, I'll be out in the garden.
And I'll slip up to town any day, if you want me.
In fact, Mrs. E. said: 'I wish he'd ring us up!
I'm sure he has a very cultivated voice.'

COLBY

Thank you very much, I will. It's reassuring
To know that I have you always at my back
If I get into trouble. But I hope
That I shan't have to call upon you often.

EGGERSON

Oh, I forgot . . . Mrs. E. keeps saying:
'Why don't you ask him out to dinner one Sunday?'
But I say: 'We couldn't ask him to come
All the way to Joshua Park, at this time of year!'
I said: 'Let's think about it in the Spring
When the garden will really be a treat to look at.'
Well, I'll be going.

SIR CLAUDE
Goodbye, and thank you, Eggerson.

EGGERSON
Good day, Sir Claude. Good day, Mr. Simpkins.

[*Exit* EGGERSON]

SIR CLAUDE

Well, Colby! I've been calling you Mr. Simpkins
In public, till now, as a matter of prudence.
As we arranged. But after two months —
And as my wife insists upon your being Mr. Colby —
I shall begin to call you Colby with everyone.

COLBY

I'm sure that will make it easier for both of us.

SIR CLAUDE

Her sudden arrival was very disconcerting:
As you gather, such a thing never happened before.
So the meeting didn't go quite the way I intended;
And yet I believe that it's all for the best.
It went off very well. It's very obvious
That she took to you at once.

COLBY

                                        Did she really think
That she had seen me before?

SIR CLAUDE

                                        Impossible to tell.
The point is that she's taken a fancy to you
And so she lays claim to you. That's very satisfactory.
She's taken it for granted that you should have the flat —
By tomorrow she'll be sure it was she who proposed it.
So I feel pretty confident that, before long,
We can put matters onto a permanent basis.

COLBY

I must confess, that up to this point
I haven't been able to feel very settled.
And what you've had in mind still seems to me
Like building my life upon a deception.
Do you really believe that Lady Elizabeth
Can ever accept me as if I was her son?

34

SIR CLAUDE

As if you were her son? If she comes to think of you
As the kind of man that her son would have been —
And I believe she will: though I'm perfectly convinced
That *her* son would have been a different type of person —
Then you *will* become her son, in her eyes. She's like that.
Why, it wouldn't surprise me if she came to believe
That you really are her son, instead of being mine.
She has always lived in a world of make-believe,
And the best one can do is to guide her delusions
In the right direction.

COLBY

                    It doesn't seem quite honest.
If we all have to live in a world of make-believe,
Is that good for us? Or a kindness to her?

SIR CLAUDE

If you haven't the strength to impose your own terms
Upon life, you must accept the terms it offers you.
But tell me first — I've a reason for asking —
How do you like your work? You don't find it uncongenial?
I'm not changing the subject: I'm coming back to it.
You know I've deliberately left you alone,
And so far we've discussed only current business,
Thinking that you might find it easier
To start by a rather formal relationship
In adapting yourself to a new situation.

COLBY

I'm very grateful to you, for that:
It is indeed a new and strange situation,
And nothing about it is real to me yet.

SIR CLAUDE

But now I want it to be different. It's odd, Colby.
I didn't realise, till you started with me here,
That we hardly know each other at all.

35

COLBY

I suppose there hasn't been the opportunity.

SIR CLAUDE

When you were a child, you belonged to your aunt,
Or·so she made me feel. I never saw you·alone.
And then when I sent you both over to Canada
In the war — that was perhaps a mistake,
Though it seemed to have such obvious advantages
That I had no doubts at the time — that's five years;
And then your school, and your military service,
And then your absorption in your music . . .

COLBY

You started by asking me how I found this work.

SIR CLAUDE

Yes, how do you find it?

COLBY

                    In a way, exhilarating.
To find there is something that I can do
So remote from my previous interests.
It gives me, in a way, a kind of self-confidence
I've never had before. Yet at the same time
It's rather disturbing. I don't mean the work:
I mean, about myself. As if I was becoming
A different person. Just as, I suppose,
If you learn to speak a foreign language fluently,
So that you can think in it — you feel yourself to be
Rather a different person when you're talking it.
I'm not at all sure that I like the other person
That I feel myself becoming — though he fascinates me.
And yet from time to time, when I least expect it,
When my mind is cleared and empty, walking in the street
Or waking in the night, then the former person,
The person I used to be, returns to take possession:
Always, when I play to myself,

And I am again the disappointed organist,
And for the moment the thing I cannot do,
The art that I could never excel in,
Seems the one thing worth doing, the one thing
That I want to do. I have to fight that person.

SIR CLAUDE

I understand what you are saying
Much better than you think. It's my own experience
That you are repeating.

COLBY
Your own experience?

SIR CLAUDE

Yes, I did not want to be a financier.

COLBY

What did you want to do?

SIR CLAUDE
I wanted to be a potter.

COLBY

A potter!

SIR CLAUDE
A potter. When I was a boy
I loved to shape things. I loved form and colour
And I loved the material that the potter handles.
Most people think that a sculptor or a painter
Is something more excellent to be than a potter.
Most people think of china or porcelain
As merely for use, or for decoration —
In either case, an inferior art.
For me, they are neither 'use' not 'decoration' —
That is, decoration as a background for living;
For me, they are life itself. To be among such things,

If it is an escape, is escape into living,
Escape from a sordid world to a pure one.
Sculpture and painting — I have some good things —
But they haven't this . . . remoteness I have always longed
    for.
I want a world where the form is the reality,
Of which the substantial is only a shadow.
It's strange. I have never talked of this to anyone.
Never until now. Do you feel at all like that
When you are alone with your music?

COLBY

                          Just the same.
All the time you've been speaking, I've been translating
Into terms of music. But may I ask,
With this passion for . . . ceramics, how did it happen
That you never made it your profession?

SIR CLAUDE

Family pressure, in the first place.
My father — your grandfather — built up this business
Starting from nothing. It was *his* passion.
He loved it with the same devotion
That I gave to clay, and what could be done with it —
What I hoped I could do with it. I thought I despised him
When I was young. And yet I was in awe of him.
I was wrong, in both. I loathed this occupation
Until I began to feel my power in it.
The life changed me, as it is changing you:
It begins as a kind of make-believe
And the make-believing makes it real.
That's not the whole story. My father knew I hated it:
That was a grief to him. He knew, I am sure,
That I cherished for a long time a secret reproach:
But after his death, and then it was too late,
I knew that he was right. And all my life
I have been atoning. To a dead father,
Who had always been right. I never understood him.

38

I was too young. And when I was mature enough
To understand him, he was not there.

You've still not explained why you came to think
That your father had been right.

                              Because I came to see
That I should never have become a first-rate potter.
I didn't have it in me. It's strange, isn't it,
That a man should have a consuming passion
To do something for which he lacks the capacity?
Could a man be said to have a vocation
To be a second-rate potter? To be, at best,
A competent copier, possessed by the craving
To create, when one is wholly uncreative?
I don't think so. For I came to see
That I had always known, at the secret moments,
That I didn't have it in me. There are occasions
When I am transported — a different person,
Transfigured in the vision of some marvellous creation,
And I feel what the man must have felt when he made it.
But nothing *I* made ever gave me that contentment —
That state of utter exhaustion and peace
Which comes in dying to give something life . . .
I intend that you shall have a good piano. The best.
And when you are alone at your piano, in the evening,
I believe you will go through the private door
Into the real world, as I do, sometimes.

Indeed, I have felt, while you've been talking,
That it's my own feelings you have expressed,
Although the medium is different. I know
I should never have become a great organist,
As I aspired to be. I'm not an executant;
I'm only a shadow of the great composers.
Always when I play to myself,

I hear the music I should like to have written,
As the composer heard it when it came to him;
But when I played before other people
I was always conscious that what *they* heard
Was not what I hear when I play to myself.
What I hear is a great musician's music,
What they hear is an inferior rendering.
So I've given up trying to play to other people:
I am only happy when I play to myself.

SIR CLAUDE

You shall play to yourself. And as for me,
I keep my pieces in a private room.
It isn't that I don't want anyone to see them!
But when I am alone, and look at one thing long enough,
I sometimes have that sense of identification
With the maker, of which I spoke — an agonising ecstasy
Which makes life bearable. It's all I have.
I suppose it takes the place of religion:
Just as my wife's investigations
Into what she calls the life of the spirit
Are a kind of substitute for religion.
I dare say truly religious people —
I've never known any — can find some unity.
Then there are also the men of genius.
There are others, it seems to me, who have at best to live
In two worlds — each a kind of make-believe.
That's you and me. Some day, perhaps,
I will show you my collection.

COLBY

Thank you.

SIR CLAUDE

And perhaps, some time, you will let me hear you play.
I shan't mention it again. I'll wait until you ask me.
Do you understand now what I meant when I spoke
Of accepting the terms life imposes upon you
Even to the point of accepting . . . make-believe?

COLBY

I think I do. At least, I understand *you* better
In learning to understand the conditions
Which life has imposed upon you. But . . . something in me
Rebels against accepting such conditions.
It would be so much simpler if you *weren't* my father!
I was struck by what you said, a little while ago,
When you spoke of never having understood your father
Until it was too late. And you spoke of atonement.
Even your failure to understand him,
Of which you spoke — that was a relationship
Of father and son. It must often happen.
And the reconcilement, after his death,
That perfects the relation. You have always been his son
And he is still your father. I only wish
That I had something to atone for!
There's something lacking between you and me,
That you had, and have, and always will have, with your
       father.
I begin to see how I have always thought of you —
As a kind of protector, a generous provider:
Rather as a patron than a father —
The father who was missing in the years of childhood.
Those years have gone forever. The empty years.
Oh, I'm terribly sorry to be saying this;
But it goes to explain what I said just now
About rebelling against the terms
That life has imposed.

SIR CLAUDE

                     It's my own fault.
I was always anxious to avoid the mistakes
My father made with me. And yet I seem
To have made a greater mistake than he did.

COLBY

I know that I'm hurting you and I know
That I hate myself for hurting you.

SIR CLAUDE

You mustn't think of that.

COLBY

I'm very grateful for all you've done for me;
And I want to do my best to justify your kindness
By the work I do.

SIR CLAUDE

As my confidential clerk.

COLBY

I'm really interested by the work I'm doing
And eager for more. I don't want my position
To be, in any way, a make-believe.

SIR CLAUDE

It shan't be. Meanwhile, we must simply wait to learn
What new conditions life will impose on us.
Just when we think we have settled our account
Life presents a new one, more difficult to pay.
— I shall go now, and sit for a while with my china.

COLBY

Excuse me, but I must remind you:
You have that meeting in the City
Tomorrow morning. You asked me to prepare
Some figures for you. I've got them here.

SIR CLAUDE

Much depends on my wife. Be patient with her, Colby.
— Oh yes that meeting. We must run through the figures.

CURTAIN

Act Two

The flat in the mews a few weeks later. COLBY *is seated at the*
piano; LUCASTA *in an armchair. The concluding bars*
of a piece of music are heard as the curtain rises.

LUCASTA

I think you play awfully well, Colby —
Not that *my* opinion counts for anything:
You know that. But I'd like to learn about music.
I wish you would teach me how to appreciate it.

COLBY

I don't think that you'll need much teaching;
Not at this stage, anyway. All you need at first
Is to hear more music. And to find out what you like.
When you know what you like, and begin to know it well,
Then you want to learn about its structure
And the various forms, and the different ways of playing it.

LUCASTA

But suppose I only like the wrong things?

COLBY

No, I'm sure you'll prefer the right things, when you hear
    them.
I've given you a test. Several of the pieces
That I've just played you were very second-rate,
And you didn't like them. You liked the right ones.

LUCASTA

Colby, I didn't know you were so artful!

So the things I liked were the right ones to like?
Still, I'm awfully ignorant. Can you believe
That I've never been to a concert in my life?
I only go to shows when somebody invites me,
And no one has ever asked me to a concert.
I've been to the Opera, of course, several times,
But I'm afraid I never really listened to the music:
I just enjoyed going — to see the other people,
And to be seen there! And because you feel out of it
If you never go to the Opera, in the season.
Though I've always felt out of it. And can you realise
That nobody has ever played to me before?

COLBY

And this is the first time I've played to anyone . . .

LUCASTA

Don't be such a fraud. You know you told me
The piano was only delivered this week
And you had it tuned yesterday. Still, I'm flattered
To be your first visitor in this flat
And to be the first to hear you play *this* piano.

COLBY

That's not what I meant. I mean that I've not played
To anyone, since I came to the conclusion
That I should never become a musician.

LUCASTA

Did you find it a strain, then, playing to me?

COLBY

As a matter of fact, I think I played better.
I can't bring myself to play to other people,
And when I'm alone I can't forget
That it's only myself to whom I'm playing.
But with you, it was neither solitude nor . . . people.

44

LUCASTA

I'm glad I'm not people. Will you play to me again
And teach me about music?

COLBY

                    Yes, of course I will.
But I'm sure that when you learn about music —
And that won't take you long — and hear good performers,
You'll very quickly realise how bad my playing is.

LUCASTA

Really, Colby, you do make difficulties!
But what about taking me to a concert?

COLBY

Only the other day, I invited you . . .

LUCASTA

To go to see that American Musical!

COLBY

Well, I'd heard you say you wanted to see it.

LUCASTA

But not with you!

COLBY

                    You made that very clear.
But why not with me?

LUCASTA

                    Because you don't like them —
American Musicals. Do you think it's any compliment
To invite a woman to something she would like
When she knows *you* wouldn't like it? That's not a compli-
        ment:
That's just being . . . patronising. But if you invite me
To something you like — that *is* a compliment.
It shows you want to educate me.

COLBY

But I didn't know
That you wanted to be educated.

LUCASTA

Neither did I.
But I wanted you to want to educate me;
And now I'm beginning to believe that I want it.

COLBY

Well, I'm going to invite you to the next concert . . .

LUCASTA

The next that you want to go to *yourself*.

COLBY

And perhaps you'll let me tell you beforehand
About the programme — or the things I want to hear.
I'll play you the themes, so you'll recognise them.
Better still, I'll play you the gramophone records.

LUCASTA

I'd rather you played me bits yourself, and explained them.
We'll begin my education at once.

COLBY

I suspect that it's you who are educating *me*.

LUCASTA

Colby, you really are full of surprises!
I've never met a man so ignorant as you
Yet knowing so much that one wouldn't suspect.
Perhaps that's why I like you.

COLBY

That's not quite the reason.

LUCASTA

Oh, so you believe that I like you?
I didn't know that you were so conceited.

46

COLBY

No, it's not conceit — the reason that I'm thinking of.
It's something quite simple.

LUCASTA

Then I wish you'd tell me.
Because *I* don't know.

COLBY

The first time we met
You were trying very hard to give a false impression.
And then you came to see that you hadn't succeeded.

LUCASTA

Oh, so I was trying to give a false impression?
What sort of impression was I trying to give?

COLBY

That doesn't really matter. But, for some reason,
You thought I'd get a false impression anyway.
You preferred it to be one of your own creation
Rather than wait to see what happened.
I hope you don't mind: I know it sounds impertinent.

LUCASTA

Well, there's one thing you haven't learnt yet,
And that is, to know when you're paying a compliment.
That was a compliment. And a very clever one.

COLBY

I admit that at first I was very bewildered
By you . . . and B.

LUCASTA

Oh, by me . . . and B.

COLBY

Only afterwards,

When I had seen you a number of times,
I decided that was only your kind of self-defence.

LUCASTA
What made you think it was self-defence?

COLBY
Because you couldn't wait to see what happened.
You're afraid of what would happen if you left things to
    themselves.
You jump — because you're afraid of being pushed.
I think that you're brave — and I think that you're fright-
    ened.
Perhaps you've been very badly hurt, at some time.
Or at least, there may have been something in your life
To rob you of any sense of security.

LUCASTA
And I'm sure you have *that* — the sense of security.

COLBY
No, I haven't either.

LUCASTA
          There, I don't believe you.
What did I think till now? Oh, its strange, isn't it,
That as one gets to know a person better
One finds them in some ways very like oneself,
In unexpected ways. And then you begin
To discover differences inside the likeness.
You may *feel* insecure, in some ways —
But your insecurity is nothing like mine.

COLBY
In what ways is it different?

LUCASTA
          It's hard to explain.
Perhaps it's something that your music stands for.

There's one thing I know. When you first told me
What a disaster it was in your life
When you found that you'd never be a good musician —
Of course, *I* don't know whether you were right.
For all I can tell, you may have been mistaken,
And perhaps you could be a very great musician:
But that's not the point. You'd convinced yourself;
And you felt that your life had all collapsed
And that you must learn to do something different.
And so you applied for Eggerson's position,
And made up your mind to go into business
And be someone like Claude . . . or B. I was sorry,
Very sorry for you. I admired your courage
In facing facts — or the facts as you saw them.
And yet, all the time, I found I *envied* you
And I didn't know why! And now I think I know.
It's awful for a man to have to give up,
A career that he's set his heart on, I'm sure:
But it's only the outer world that you've lost:
You've still got your inner world — a world that's more real.
That's why you're different from the rest of us:
You have your secret garden; to which you can retire
And lock the gate behind you.

COLBY

                    And lock the gate behind me?
Are you sure that you haven't your own secret garden
Somewhere, if you could find it?

LUCASTA

                    If I could find it!
No, my only garden is . . . a dirty public square
In a shabby part of London — like the one where I lived
For a time, with my mother. I've no garden.
I hardly feel that I'm even a person:
Nothing but a bit of living matter
Floating on the surface of the Regent's Canal.
Floating, that's it.

49

COLBY

You're very much a person.
I'm sure that there is a garden somewhere for you —
For anyone who wants one as much as you do.

LUCASTA

And *your* garden is a garden
Where you hear a music that no one else could hear,
And the flowers have a scent that no one else could smell.

COLBY

You may be right, up to a point.
And yet, you know, it's not quite real to me —
Although it's as real to me as . . . this world.
But that's just the trouble. They seem so unrelated.
I turn the key, and walk through the gate,
And there I am . . . alone, in my 'garden'.
Alone, that's the thing. That's why it's not real.
You know, I think that Eggerson's garden
Is more real than mine.

LUCASTA

Eggerson's garden?
What makes you think of Eggerson — of all people?

COLBY

Well, he retires to his garden — literally,
And also in the same sense that I retire to mine.
But he doesn't feel alone there. And when he comes out
He has marrows, or beetroot, or peas . . . for Mrs. Eggerson.

LUCASTA

Are you laughing at me?

COLBY

I'm being very serious.
What I mean is, my garden's no less unreal to me

Than the world outside it. If you have two lives
Which have nothing whatever to do with each other —
Well, they're both unreal. But for Eggerson
His garden is a part of one single world.

LUCASTA

But what do you want?

COLBY

Not to be alone there.
If I were religious, God would walk in my garden
And that would make the world outside it real
And acceptable, I think.

LUCASTA

You sound awfully religious.
Is there no other way of making it real to you?

COLBY

It's simply the fact of being alone there
That makes it unreal.

LUCASTA

Can no one else enter?

COLBY

It can't be done by issuing invitations:
They would just have to come. And I should not see them
        coming.
I should not hear the opening of the gate.
They would simply . . . be there suddenly,
Unexpectedly. Walking down an alley
I should become aware of someone walking with me.
That's the only way I can think of putting it.

LUCASTA

How afraid one is of . . . being hurt!

COLBY

It's not the hurting that one would mind
But the sense of desolation afterwards.

LUCASTA

I know what you mean. Then the flowers would fade
And the music would stop. And the walls would be broken.
And you would find yourself in a devastated area —
A bomb-site . . . willow-herb . . . a dirty public square.
But I can't imagine that happening to you.
You seem so secure, to me. Not only in your music —
That's just its expression. You don't seem to me
To need anybody.

COLBY

That's quite untrue.

LUCASTA

But you've something else, that I haven't got:
Something of which the music is a . . . symbol.
I really would like to understand music,
Not in order to be able to talk about it,
But . . . partly, to enjoy it . . . and because of what it stands
    for.
You know, I'm a little jealous of your music!
When I see it as a means of contact with a world
More real than any *I've* ever lived in.
And I'd like to understand *you*.

COLBY

                    I believe you do already,
Better than . . . other people. And I want to understand *you*.
Does one ever come to understand anyone?

LUCASTA

I think you're very discouraging:
Are you doing it deliberately?

52

COLBY

That's not what I meant.
I meant, there's no end to understanding a person.
All one can do is to understand them better,
To keep up with them; so that as the other changes
You can understand the change as soon as it happens,
Though you couldn't have predicted it.

LUCASTA

I think I'm changing
I've changed quite a lot in the last two hours.

COLBY

And I think I'm changing too. But perhaps what we call
    change . . .

LUCASTA

Is understanding better what one really is.
And the reason why that comes about, perhaps . . .

COLBY

Is, beginning to understand another person.

LUCASTA

Oh Colby, now that we begin to understand,
I'd like you to know a little more about me.
You must have wondered.

COLBY

Must have wondered?
No, I haven't wondered. It's all a strange world
To me, you know, in which I find myself.
But if you mean, wondered about your . . . background:
No. I've been curious to know what you *are*,
But not who you are, in the ordinary sense.
Is that what you mean? I've just accepted you.

LUCASTA

Oh, that's so wonderful, to be accepted!

No one has ever 'just accepted' me before.
Of course the facts don't matter, in a sense.
But now we've got to this point — you might as well know
    them.

COLBY

I'd gladly tell you everything about myself;
But you know most of what there is to say
Already, either from what I've told you
Or from what I've told B.; or from Sir Claude.

LUCASTA

Claude hasn't told me anything about you;
He doesn't tell me much. And as for B. —
I'd much rather hear it from yourself.

COLBY

There's only one thing I can't tell you.
At least, not yet. I'm not allowed to tell.
And that's about my parents.

LUCASTA

        Oh, I see.
Well, I can't believe that matters.
But I can tell you all about *my* parents:
At least, I'm going to.

COLBY

        Does that matter, either?

LUCASTA

In one way, it matters. A little while ago
You said, very cleverly, that when we first met
You saw I was trying to give a false impression.
I want to tell you now, why I tried to do that.
And it's always succeeded with people before:
I got into the habit of giving that impression.
That's where B. has been such a help to me —

He fosters the impression. He half believes in it.
But he knows all about me, and he knows
That what some men have thought about me wasn't true.

COLBY

What wasn't true?

LUCASTA

That I was Claude's mistress —
Or had been his mistress, palmed off on B.

COLBY

I never thought of such a thing!

LUCASTA

You never thought of such
a thing!
There are not many men who wouldn't have thought it.
I don't know about B. He's very generous.
I don't think he'd have minded. But he's very clever too;
And he guessed the truth from the very first moment.

COLBY

But what is there to know?

LUCASTA

You'll laugh when I tell you:
I'm only Claude's daughter.

COLBY

His daughter!

LUCASTA

His daughter. Oh, it's a sordid story.
I hated my mother. I never could see
How Claude had ever liked her. Oh, that childhood —
Always living in seedy lodgings
And being turned out when the neighbours complained.

55

Oh of course Claude gave her money, a regular allowance;
But it wouldn't have mattered how much he'd given her:
It was always spent before the end of the quarter
On gin and betting, I should guess.
And I knew how she supplemented her income
When I was sent out. I've been locked in a cupboard!
I was only eight years old
When she died of an 'accidental overdose'.
Then Claude took me over. That was lucky.
But I was old enough to remember . . . too much.

COLBY

You are Claude's daughter!

LUCASTA

     Oh, there's no doubt of that.
I'm sure he wished there had been. He's been good to me
In his way. But I'm always a reminder to him
Of something he would prefer to forget.
    [A pause]
But why don't you say something? Are you shocked?

COLBY

Shocked? No. Yes. You don't understand.
I want to explain. But I can't, just yet.
Oh, why did I ever come into this house!
Lucasta . . .

LUCASTA

    I can see well enough you *are* shocked.
You ought to see your face! I'm disappointed.
I suppose that's all. I believe your'e more shocked
Than if I'd told you I *was* Claude's mistress.
Claude has always been ashamed of me:
Now *you're* ashamed of me. I thought you'd understand.
Little you know what it's like to be a bastard
And wanted by nobody. I know why your'e shocked:
Claude has just accepted me like a debit item
Always in his cash account. I don't like myself.

56

I don't like the person I've forced myself to be;
And I liked you because you didn't like that person either,
And I thought you'd come to see me as the real kind of
        person
That I want to be. That I know I am.
That was new to me. I suppose I was flattered.
And I thought, now, perhaps, if someone else sees me
As I really am, I might become myself.

COLBY

Oh Lucasta, I'm not shocked. Not by you,
Not by anything you think. It's to do with myself.

LUCASTA

Yourself, indeed! Your precious self!
Why don't you shut yourself up in that garden
Where you like to be alone with yourself?
Or perhaps you think it would be bad for your prospects
Now that you're Claude's white-headed boy.
Perhaps he'll adopt you, and make you his heir
And you'll marry another Lady Elizabeth.
But in that event, Colby, you'll have to accept me
As your sister! Even if I am a guttersnipe . . .

COLBY

You mustn't use such words! You don't know how it's
        hurting.

LUCASTA

I could use words much stronger than that,
And I will, if I choose. Oh, I'm sorry:
I suppose it's my mother coming out in me.
You know, Colby, I'm truly disappointed.
I was sure, when I told you all I did,
That you wouldn't mind at all. That you might be sorry
        for me.
But now I don't want you to be sorry, thank you.
Why, I'd actually thought of telling you before,

And I postponed telling you, just for the fun of it:
I thought, when I tell him, it will be so wonderful
All in a moment. And now there's nothing,
Nothing at all. It's far worse than ever.
Just when you think you're on the point of release
From loneliness, then loneliness swoops down upon you;
When you think you're getting out, you're getting further
     in,
And you know at last that there's no escape.
Well, I'll be going.

COLBY

You mustn't go yet!
There's something else that I want to explain,
And now I'm going to. I'm breaking a promise. But . . .

LUCASTA

I don't believe there's anything to explain
That could explain anything away. I shall never
Never forget that look on your face
When I told you about Claude and my mother.
I may be a bastard, but I have some self-respect.
Well, there's always B. I think that now
I'm just beginning to appreciate B.

COLBY

Lucasta, wait!
[*Enter* B. KAGHAN]

KAGHAN

Enter B. Kaghan.
To see the new flat. And here's Lucasta.
I knew I should find she'd got in first!
Trust Kaghan's intuitions! I'm your guardian angel,
Colby, to protect your from Lucasta.

LUCASTA

You're *my* guardian angel at the moment, B.
You're to take me out to dinner. And I'm dying for a drink.

58

KAGHAN

I told Colby, never learn to mix cocktails,
If you don't want women always dropping in on you.
And between a couple of man-eating tigers
Like you and Lizzie, he's got to have protection.

LUCASTA

Colby doesn't need your protection racket
So far as I'm concerned, B. And as for Lizzie,
You'd better not get in *her* way when she's hunting.
But all that matters now is, that I'm hungry,
And you've got to give me a very good dinner.

KAGHAN

You shall be fed. All in good time.
I've come to inspect the new bachelor quarters,
And to wish Colby luck. I've always been lucky,
And I always bring luck to other people.

COLBY

Will you have a glass of sherry?

KAGHAN

                              Yes, I'll have a glass of
    sherry,
To drink success to the flat. Lucasta too:
Much better for you than cocktails, Lucasta.

LUCASTA

You know I don't like sherry.

KAGHAN

                    You've got to drink it,
To Colby, and a happy bachelor life!
Which depends, of course, on preventing Lizzie
From always interfering. Be firm with her, Colby;
Assert your right to a little privacy.
Now's the moment for firmness. Don't let her cross the
    threshold.

LUCASTA

As if you weren't as afraid of her as anybody!

KAGHAN

Well, at least, I've always managed to escape her.

LUCASTA

Only because she's never wanted to pursue you.

KAGHAN

Yes, I made a bad impression at the start:
I saw that it was necessary. I'm afraid Colby
Has made a good impression; which he'll have to live down.
— I must say, I like the way you've had the place done up.

COLBY

It was Lady Elizabeth chose the decorations.

KAGHAN

Then I'm not sure I like them. You must change the colours.
It's all a bit too dim. You need something brighter.
But otherwise, it looks pretty comfortable.
If I was as snug as Colby is, Lucasta,
I'd never have thought of changing my condition.

LUCASTA

You're always free to think again.

KAGHAN

Marriage is a gamble. But I'm a born gambler
And I've put my shirt . . . no, not quite the right expression—
Lucasta's the most exciting speculation
I've ever thought of investing in.
Colby's more cautious. You know, Colby,
You and I ought to be in business together.
I'm a good guesser. But I sometimes guess wrong.
I make decisions on the spur of the moment,
But you'd never take a leap in the dark;
You'd keep me on the rails.

COLBY

That's just nonsense.
You only pretend that you're a gambler.
You've got as level a head as anyone,
And you never get involved in anything risky.
You like to pretend to other people
That you're a gambler. I don't believe you ever gamble
On anything that isn't a certainty.

KAGHAN

Well, there's something in that. You know, Lucasta,
Colby is a good judge of character.

LUCASTA

You'd need to be a better judge of character
Yourself, before you said that of Colby.

KAGHAN

Oh, I'm a good judge. Now, I'll tell you the difference
Between ourselves and Colby. You and me —
The one thing *we* want is security
And respectability! Now Colby
Doesn't really care about being respectable —
He was born and bred to it. I wasn't, Colby.
Do you know, I was a foundling? You didn't know that!
Never had any parents. Just adopted, from nowhere.
That's why I want to be a power in the City,
On the boards of all the solidest companies:
Because I've no background — no background at all.
That's one thing I like about Lucasta:
She doesn't despise me.

LUCASTA

Nobody could despise you.
And what's more important, you don't despise *me*.

KAGHAN

Nobody could despise *you*, Lucasta;

61

And we want the same things. But as for Colby,
He's the sort of fellow who might chuck it all
And go to live on a desert island.
But I hope you won't do that. We need you where you are.

COLBY

I'm beginning to believe you've a pretty shrewd insight
Into things that have nothing to do with business.

KAGHAN

And you have a very sound head for business.
Maybe you're a better financier than I am!
That's why we ought to be in business together.

LUCASTA

You're both very good at paying compliments;
But I remarked that I was hungry.

KAGHAN

                            You can't want dinner yet.
it's only six o'clock. We can't dine till eight;
Not at any restaurant that *you* like.
— For a change, let's talk about Lucasta.

LUCASTA
[*rising*]
If you want to discuss *me* . . .
[*A knock at the door. Enter* LADY ELIZABETH]

LADY ELIZABETH
                            Oh, good evening.
Good evening, Mr. Kaghan. Good evening, Lucasta.
Have you just arrived, or are you just leaving?

LUCASTA

We're on the point of leaving, Lady Elizabeth.

LADY ELIZABETH

I've come over to have a look at the flat

Now that you've moved in. Because you can't tell
Whether a scheme of decoration
Is *right*, until the place has been lived in
By the person for whom it was designed.
So I have to see you in it. Did you say you were leaving?

KAGHAN

We're going out to dinner. Lucasta's very hungry.

LADY ELIZABETH

Hungry? At six o'clock? Where will you get dinner?
Oh, I know. It's a chance to try that Herbal Restaurant
I recommended to you. You can have dinner early:
Most of its patrons dine at half past six.
They have the most delicious salads!
And I told you, Mr. Kaghan, you're the type of person
Who needs to eat a great deal of salad.
You remember, I made you take a note of the address;
And I don't believe that you've been there yet.

KAGHAN

Why no, as a matter of fact, I haven't.
I've kept meaning to. Shall we go there, Lucasta?

LUCASTA

I'm so hungry, I could even eat a herbal salad.

LADY ELIZABETH

That's right. Just mention my name, Mr. Kaghan,
And ask for the table in the left hand corner:
It has the best waitress. Good night.

LUCASTA

Good night.

KAGHAN

And thank you so much. You give such good advice.
                    [*Exeunt* KAGHAN *and* LUCASTA]
63

LADY ELIZABETH

Were those young people here by appointment?
Or did they come in unexpectedly?

COLBY

I'd invited Lucasta. She had asked me to play to her.

LADY ELIZABETH

You call her Lucasta? Young people nowadays
Seem to have dropped the use of surnames altogether.
But, Colby, I hope you won't mind a gentle hint.
I feared it was possible you might become too friendly
With Mr. Kaghan and Miss Angel.
I can see you've lived a rather sheltered life,
And I've noticed them paying you a good deal of attention.
You see, you're rather a curiosity
To both of them — you're not the sort of person
They ever meet in their kind of society.
So naturally, they want to take you up.
I can speak more freely, as an elderly person.

COLBY

But, Lady Elizabeth . . .

LADY ELIZABETH

                    Well, older than you are,
And a good deal wiser in the ways of the world.

COLBY

But, Lady Elizabeth, what is it you object to?
They're both intelligent . . . and kind.

LADY ELIZABETH

Oh, I don't say they're not intelligent and kind.
I'm not making any malicious suggestions:
But they are rather worldly and materialistic,
And . . . well, rather vulgar. They're not your sort at all.

COLBY

I shouldn't call them vulgar. Perhaps I'm vulgar too.
But what, do you think, *is* my sort?
I don't know, myself. And I should like to know.

LADY ELIZABETH

In the first place, you ought to mix with people of breeding.
I said to myself, when I first saw you,
'He is very well bred'. I knew nothing about you,
But one doesn't need to know, if one knows what breeding is.
And, second, you need intellectual society.
Now, that already limits your acquaintance:
Because, what's surprising, well-bred people
Are sometimes far from intellectual;
And — what's less surprising — intellectual people
Are often ill-bred. But that's not all.
You need intellectual, well-bred people
Of spirituality — and that's the rarest.

COLBY

That would limit my acquaintance to a very small number,
And I don't know where to find them.

LADY ELIZABETH

                       They can be found.
But I came to have a look at the flat
To see if the colour scheme really suited you.
I believe it does. The walls; and the curtains;
And most of the furniture. But, that writing-table!
Where did that writing-table come from?

COLBY

It's an office desk. Sir Claude got it for me.
I said I needed a desk in my room:
You see, I shall do a good deal of my work here.

LADY ELIZABETH

And what is that shrouded object on it?
Don't tell me it's a typewriter.

COLBY

It is a typewriter.
I've already begun to work here. At the moment
I'm working on a company report.

LADY ELIZABETH

I hadn't reckoned on reports and typewriters
When I designed this room.

COLBY

It's the sort of room I wanted.

LADY ELIZABETH
[*rising*]
And I see a photograph in a silver frame.
I'm afraid I shall have to instruct you, Colby.
Photographic portraits — even in silver frames —
Are much too intimate for the sitting-room.
May I remove it? Surely your bedroom
Is the proper place for photographic souvenirs.
[*She sits down, holding the portrait*]
What was I going to say? Oh, I know.
Do you believe in reincarnation?

COLBY

No, I don't. I mean, I've never thought about it.

LADY ELIZABETH

I can't say that *I* believe in it.
I did, for a time. I studied the doctrine.
But I was going to say, *if* I believed in it
I should have said that we had known each other
In some previous incarnation. — Is this your mother?

COLBY

No, that is my aunt. I never knew my mother.
She died when I was born.

LADY ELIZABETH

                    She died when you were born.
Have you other near relatives? Brothers or sisters?

COLBY

No brothers or sisters. No. As for other relatives,
I never knew any, when I was a child.
I suppose I've never been interested . . . in relatives.

LADY ELIZABETH

You did not want to know your relatives!
I understand exactly how you felt.
How I disliked my parents! I had a governess;
Several, in fact. And I loathed them all.   .
Were you brought up by a governess?

COLBY

                    No. By my aunt.

LADY ELIZABETH

And did you loathe her? No, of course not.
Or you wouldn't have her portrait. If you never knew your
          parents . . .
But was your father living?

COLBY

                    I never knew my father.

LADY ELIZABETH

Then, if you never had a governess,
And if you never knew either of your parents,
You can't understand what loathing really is.
Yet we must have *some* similarity of background.

COLBY

But you had parents. And no doubt, many relatives.

LADY ELIZABETH

Oh, swarms of relatives! And such unpleasant people!

I thought of myself as a dove in an eagle's nest.
They were so carnivorous. Always killing things and eating
    them.
And yet our childhood must have been similar.
These are only superficial differences:
You must have been a lonely child, having no relatives —
No brothers or sisters — and I was lonely
Because they were so numerous — and so uncongenial.
They made me feel an outcast. And yet they were so
    commonplace.
Do you know, Colby, when I was a child
I had three obsessions, and I never told anyone.
I wonder if *you* had the same obsessions?

COLBY

What were they?

LADY ELIZABETH
           The first was, that I was very ugly
And didn't know it. Then, that I was feeble-minded
And didn't know it. Finally,
That I was a foundling, and didn't know it.
Of course, I was terrified of being ugly,
And of being feeble-minded: though my family made me
    think so.
But you know, I actually *liked* to believe
That I was a foundling — or do I mean 'changeling'?

COLBY

I don't know which you mean.

LADY ELIZABETH
           However that may be,
I didn't want to belong there. I refused to believe
That my father could have been an ordinary earl!
And I couldn't believe that my mother *was* my mother.
These were foolish fancies. I was a silly girl,
And very romantic. But it goes to show

How different I felt myself to be.
And then I took up the Wisdom of the East
And believed, for a while, in reincarnation.
That seemed to explain it all. I don't believe it now.
That was only a phase. But it made it all so simple!
To be able to think that one's earthly parents
Are only the means that we have to employ
To become reincarnate. And that one's real ancestry
Is one's previous existences. Of course, there's something in
    us,
In all of us, which isn't just heredity,
But something unique. Something we have been
From eternity. Something . . . straight from God.
That means that we are nearer to God than to anyone.
— Where did you live, as a child?

COLBY

In Teddington.

LADY ELIZABETH

Teddington? In what county?

COLBY

It's very close to London.

LADY ELIZABETH

Still, you were brought up, like me, in the country.
Teddington. I seem to have heard of it.
Was it a large house?

COLBY

No, a very small one.

LADY ELIZABETH

But you had your aunt. And she was devoted to you,
I have no doubt. What is your aunt's name?
Is it Simpkins?

COLBY

No, a married aunt.
A widow. Her name is Mrs. Guzzard.

LADY ELIZABETH

Guzzard? Did you say Guzzard? An unusual name.
Guzzard, did you say? The name means something to me.
Yes. Guzzard. *That* is the name I've been hunting for!

COLBY

You may have come across the name before;
Although, as you say, it is an uncommon one.
You couldn't have known my aunt.

LADY ELIZABETH

                              No. I never met . . . your
    aunt.
But the name is familiar. How old are you, Colby?

COLBY

I'm twenty-five.

LADY ELIZABETH

                  Twenty-five. What became of your father?

COLBY

Well . . . I didn't have a father.
You see . . . I was an illegitimate child.

LADY ELIZABETH

Oh yes. An illegitimate child.
So that the only relative you knew
Was Mrs. Guzzard. And you always called her 'aunt'?

COLBY

Why not? She was my aunt.

LADY ELIZABETH

And as for your mother —
Mrs. Guzzard's sister, I suppose . . .

COLBY

Her sister — which makes Mrs. Guzzard my aunt.

LADY ELIZABETH

And are you quite sure that Mrs. Guzzard's sister —
Who you say was your mother — really was your mother?

COLBY

Why, Lady Elizabeth! Why should I doubt it?
That is not the kind of story my aunt would invent.

LADY ELIZABETH

Not if she *is* your aunt. Did Mrs. Guzzard
And Mr. Guzzard — have any children?

COLBY

They had no children of their own.
That is to say, they had had one little boy
Who died when I was very young indeed.
I don't remember him. I was told about him.
But I can't help wondering why you are so interested:
There's nothing very interesting about my background —
I assure you there isn't.

LADY ELIZABETH

It may be more interesting
Than you are aware of. Colby . . .
[*A knock on the door*]
Who's that?
[*Enter* SIR CLAUDE]

SIR CLAUDE

Elizabeth! I was told that you were here with Colby.
So I came over instead of telephoning,

Just to give him these notes. They're notes for my speech
At the dinner of the Potters' Company.

COLBY

That's tomorrow night, I believe.

SIR CLAUDE
                              Yes it is.
But you know that I'll have to have my speech written out
And then memorise it. I can't use notes:
It's got to sound spontaneous. I've jotted down some
          headings.
Just see if you can develop them for me
With a few striking phrases. It should last about ten minutes.
And then we'll go over it tomorrow.

COLBY
[*looking at the notes*]
                              I'll try.

SIR CLAUDE

It's just in ways like this, Elizabeth,
That Colby can be of greater help than Eggerson.
I couldn't have asked Eggerson to write a speech for me.
Oh, by the way, Colby, how's the piano?

COLBY

It's a wonderful piano. I've never played
On such an instrument. It's much too good for me.

SIR CLAUDE

You need a good piano. You'll play all the better.

LADY ELIZABETH

Claude!

SIR CLAUDE
What is it, Elizabeth?

72

LADY ELIZABETH

I've just made a startling discovery!
All through a name — and intuition.
But it shall be proved. The truth has **come out.**
It's Colby. Colby is my lost child!

SIR CLAUDE

What? Your child, Elizabeth? What on earth makes you
    think so?

LADY ELIZABETH

I must see this Mrs. Guzzard. I must confront her.
This couldn't possibly be a coincidence.
It seems incredible, doesn't it, Claude?
And yet it would be still more credible
If it were only a coincidence.
Perhaps I ought not to believe it yet,
Perhaps it is wrong of me to feel so sure,
But it seems that Providence has brought you back to me,
And you, Claude, and Eggerson have been the instruments.
I must be right. Claude, tell me I am right.

SIR CLAUDE

But Elizabeth, what has led you to believe
That Colby is your son?

LADY ELIZABETH

        Oh, I forgot
In my excitement: you arrived the very moment
When the truth dawned on me. Mrs. Guzzard!
Claude, Colby was brought up by a Mrs. Guzzard.

SIR CLAUDE

I know that. But why should that make him your son?

LADY ELIZABETH

It's the name I've been hunting for all these years —
That, and the other name, *Teddington*:

Mrs. Guzzard of Teddington. That was all I knew.
Then Tony was killed, as you know, in Africa,
And I had lost the name. Mrs. Guzzard.

SIR CLAUDE

I'm beginning now to piece it together.
You've been asking Colby about his family . . .

LADY ELIZABETH

And when he mentioned *Teddington*, there was a faint echo
And then Mrs. Guzzard! It must be true.

SIR CLAUDE

It is certainly a remarkable coincidence —
If it is a coincidence. But I'm afraid, Elizabeth,
What has happened is that, brooding on the past,
You began to think of Colby as what your son would be,
And then you began to see him as your son,
And then — any name you heard would have seemed the
    right one.

LADY ELIZABETH

Oh Claude, how can you be so sceptical!
We must see this Mrs. Guzzard, and get her to confess it.

SIR CLAUDE

I'm sorry, Elizabeth. If Mrs. Guzzard comes
To make her confession, it will be very different
From what you expect. I'm afraid, Colby,
It seems to me that we must let her know the truth.

COLBY

It seems to me . . . there is nothing for me —
Absolutely nothing — for me to say about it.
I must leave that to you.

SIR CLAUDE

       I should have told you one day.

I've always loathed keeping such a thing from you.
I see now I might as well have told you before,
But I'd hoped — and now it seems a silly thought . . .
What happens is so like what one had planned for,
And yet such a travesty of all one's plans —
I'd hoped that you would become fond of Colby,
And that he might come to take the place of your own child,
If you got to know him first — and that you'd want to adopt
    him.

LADY ELIZABETH

But of course I want to adopt him, Claude!
That is, if one's allowed to adopt one's own child.

SIR CLAUDE

That's not what I meant. Elizabeth,
Colby is *my* son.

LADY ELIZABETH

        Quite impossible, Claude!
You have a daughter. Now you want a son.

SIR CLAUDE

I'd never want to take your son away from you.
Perhaps you have a son. But it isn't Colby.
I ought to have told you, years ago.
I told you about Lucasta, and you told me
About your own . . . misfortune. And I almost told you
About Colby. I didn't. For such a foolish reason.
Absurd it sounds now. One child each —
That seemed fair enough — though yours had been lost,
And mine I couldn't lose. But if I had another
I thought you might think — 'and how many more?'
You might have suspected any number of children!
That seems grotesque now. But it influenced me.
And I found a better reason for keeping silent.
I came to see how you longed for a son of your own,
And I thought, I'll wait for children of *our* own,

75

And tell her then. And they never came.
And now I regret the decision bitterly.
I ought to have told you that I had a son.

LADY ELIZABETH
But why do you think that Colby is your son?

SIR CLAUDE
Colby is the son of Mrs. Guzzard's sister,
Who died when he was born. Mrs. Guzzard brought him up,
And I provided for his education.
I have watched him grow. And Mrs. Guzzard
Knows he is my son.

LADY ELIZABETH
                    But where were you, Claude,
When Colby was born?

SIR CLAUDE
                    Where was I? In Canada.
My father had sent me on a business tour
To learn about his overseas investments.

LADY ELIZABETH
Then how do you know that the sister had a child?
Perhaps Mrs. Guzzard invented the story. . . .

SIR CLAUDE
Why should she invent it? The child was expected.

LADY ELIZABETH
In order to get money from you, perhaps.
No, I shouldn't say that. But she had a child
Left on her hands. The father had died
And she'd never been told the name of the mother;
And the mother had forgotten the name of Mrs. Guzzard,
And I was the mother and the child was Colby;
And Mrs. Guzzard thought you would be happy

To think you had a son, and would do well by him —
Because you *did* care for the girl, didn't you?

SIR CLAUDE

Yes, I did care. Very much. I had never
Been in love before.

LADY ELIZABETH

Very well then.
That is the way it must have happened.
Oh, Claude, you know I'm rather weak in the head
Though I try to be clever. Do try to help me.

SIR CLAUDE

It could have happened. But I'm sure it didn't.

LADY ELIZABETH

Oh, Colby, doesn't your instinct tell you?

SIR CLAUDE

Yes, tell us everything that's in your mind.
I know this situation must be more of an agony
To You, than it can be even to . . . us.

COLBY

I only wish it was more acute agony:
I don't know whether I've been suffering or not
During this conversation. I only feel . . . numb.
If there's agony, it's part of a total agony
Which I can't begin to feel yet. I'm simply indifferent.
And all the time that you've been talking
I've only been thinking: 'What does it matter
Whose son I am?' You don't understand
That when one has lived without parents, as a child,
There's a gap that never can be filled. Never.
I like you both, I could even come to love you —
But as friends . . . older friends. Neither, as a parent.
I am sorry. But that's why I say it doesn't matter
To me, which of you should be my parent.

77

LADY ELIZABETH

But a mother, Colby, isn't that different?
There should always be a bond between mother and son,
No matter how long they have lost each other.

COLBY

No, Lady Elizabeth. The position is the same
Or crueller. Suppose I am your son.
Then it's merely a fact. Better not know
Than to know the fact and know it means nothing.
At the time I was born, you might have been my mother,
But you chose not to be. I don't blame you for that:
God forbid! but we must take the consequences.
At the time when I was born, your being my mother —
If you are my mother — was a living fact.
Now, it is a dead fact, and out of dead facts
Nothing living can spring. Now, it is too late.
I never wanted a parent till now —
I never thought about it. Now, you have made me think,
And I wish that I could have had a father and a mother.

LADY ELIZABETH

Stop, Colby! Something has come to me.
Claude! I don't want to take away from you
The son you thought was yours. And I know from what you
        said,
That you would rather he was *ours* than only *yours*.
Why should we make any further enquiries?
Let us regard him as being *our* son:
It won't be the same as what we had wanted —
But in some ways better! And prevent us both
From making unreasonable claims upon you, Colby.
It's a good idea! Why should we not be happy,
All of us? Already, Claude,
I feel as if this brought us closer together.

SIR CLAUDE

I should be contented with such an understanding;

And indeed, it's not so far from what I had intended.
Could you accept us both in that way, Colby?

COLBY

I can only say what I feel at the moment:
And yet I believe I shall always feel the same.

SIR CLAUDE

Well?

COLBY

It would be easier, I think,
To accept you both in the place of parents
If neither of you could be. If it was pure fiction —
One can live on a fiction — but not on such a mixture
Of fiction and fact. Already, it's been hard
For me, who have never known the feelings of a son,
To be disputed between two parents.
But, if we followed your suggestion,
I know, I know I should always be haunted
By the miserable ghosts of the other parents!
It's strange enough to have two parents —
But I should have four! What about those others?
I should have to live with those ghosts, one indignant
At being cheated of his — or her — parenthood,
The other indignant at the imputation
Of false parenthood. Both mocked at.

SIR CLAUDE

Then what do you want, Colby? What do you want?
Think of the future. When you marry
You will want parents, for the sake of your children.

COLBY

I don't feel, tonight, that I ever want to marry.
You may be right. I can't take account of that.
But now I want to know whose son I am.

79

SIR CLAUDE

Then the first thing is: we must see Mrs. Guzzard.

LADY ELIZABETH

Oh Claude! I am terribly sorry for you.
I believe that if I had known of your . . . delusion
I would never have undeceived you.

SIR CLAUDE

                    And as for me,
If I could have known what was going to happen,
I would gladly have surrendered Colby to you.
But we must see Mrs. Guzzard. I'll arrange to get her here.

LADY ELIZABETH

And I think you ought to get Eggerson as well.

SIR CLAUDE
[*rising*]
Oh, of course, Eggerson! He knows all about it.
Let us say no more tonight. Now, Colby,
Can you find some consolation at the piano?

COLBY

I don't think, tonight, the piano would help me:
At the moment, I never want to touch it again.
But there's another reason. I must remind you
About your speech for the Potters' Company
Tomorrow night. I must get to work on it.

SIR CLAUDE

Tomorrow night. Must I go to that dinner
Tomorrow night?

COLBY

              I was looking at your notes —
Before you brought me into the conversation —
And I found one note I couldn't understand.

'Reminiscent mood.' I can't develop that
Unless you can tell me — reminiscent of what?

SIR CLAUDE

Reminiscent of what? Reminiscent of what?
'Tonight I feel in a reminiscent mood' —
Oh yes. To say something of my early ambitions
To be a potter. Not that the Members
Of the Potters' Company know anything at all
About ceramics . . . or any other art.
No, I don't think I shall be in a reminiscent mood.
Cross that out. It would only remind me
Of things that would surprise the Potters' Company
If I told them what I was really remembering.
Come, Elizabeth.

LADY ELIZABETH
My poor Claude!

[*Exeunt* SIR CLAUDE *and* LADY ELIZABETH]

CURTAIN

Act Three

The Business Room, as in Act 1. *Several mornings later.* SIR
      CLAUDE *is moving chairs about. Enter* LADY ELIZA-
      BETH.

LADY ELIZABETH

Claude, what are you doing?

SIR CLAUDE

                    Settling the places.
It's important, when you have a difficult meeting,
To decide on the seating arrangements beforehand.
I don't think you and I should be near together.
Will you sit there, beside the desk?

LADY ELIZABETH

On the other side, with the light behind me:
But won't you be sitting at the desk yourself?

SIR CLAUDE

No, that would look too formal. I thought it would be better
To put Eggerson there, behind the desk.
You see, I want him to be a sort of chairman.

LADY ELIZABETH

That's a good idea.

SIR CLAUDE

                    On the other hand,
We mustn't look like a couple of barristers
Ready to cross-examine a witness.
It's very awkward. We don't want to start

By offending Mrs. Guzzard. That's why I thought
That Eggerson should put the first questions.
He's very good at approaching a subject
In a roundabout way. But where shall we place her?

LADY ELIZABETH

Over there, with the light full on her:
I want to be able to watch her expression.

SIR CLAUDE

But not in this chair! She must have an armchair . . .

LADY ELIZABETH

Not such a low one. Leave that in the corner
For Colby. He won't want to be conspicuous,
Poor boy!

SIR CLAUDE

After all, it was he who insisted
On this . . . investigation. But perhaps you're right.

LADY ELIZABETH

Claude, I've been thinking things over and over —
All through the night. I hardly slept at all.
I wish that Colby, somehow, might prove to be *your* son
Instead of mine. Really, I do!
It would be so much fairer. If he is mine —
As I'm sure he is — then you never had a son;
While, if he were yours . . . he could still take the place
Of my son: and so he could be *our* son.
Oh dear, what do I want? I should like him to be mine,
But for you to believe that he is yours!
So I hope Mrs. Guzzard will say he is your son
And I needn't believe her. I don't believe in facts.
You do. That is the difference between us.

SIR CLAUDE

I'm not so sure of that. I've tried to believe in facts;
And I've always acted as if I believed in them.

I thought it was facts that my father believed in;
I thought that what he cared for was power and wealth;
And I came to see that what I had interpreted
In this way, was something else to *him* —
An idea, an inspiration. What he wanted to transmit to me
Was that idea, that inspiration,
Which to him was life. To me, it was a burden.
You can't communicate an inspiration,
Like that, by force of will. He was a great financier —
And I am merely a successful one.
I might have been truer to my father's inspiration
If I had done what I wanted to do.

LADY ELIZABETH

You've never talked like this to me before!
Why haven't you? I don't suppose I understand
And I know you don't think I understand anything,
And perhaps I don't. But I wish you would talk
Sometimes to me as if I did understand,
And perhaps I might come to understand better.
What did you want to do?

SIR CLAUDE
                    To be a potter.

Don't laugh.

LADY ELIZABETH
            I'm not laughing. I was only thinking
How strange to have lived with you, all these years,
And now you tell me, you'd have liked to be a potter!
You really mean, to make jugs and jars
Like those in your collection?

SIR CLAUDE
                    That's what I mean.

LADY ELIZABETH

But I should have loved you to be a potter!
Why have you never told me?

SIR CLAUDE

            I didn't think
That you would be interested. More than that.
I took it for granted that what you wanted
Was a husband of importance. I thought you would despise
      me
If you knew what I'd really wanted to be.

LADY ELIZABETH

And I took it for granted that you were not interested
In anything but financial affairs;
And that you needed me chiefly as a hostess.
It's a great mistake, I do believe,
For married people to take anything for granted.

SIR CLAUDE

That was a very intelligent remark.
Perhaps I have taken too much for granted
About you, Elizabeth. What did *you* want?

LADY ELIZABETH

To inspire an artist. Don't laugh.

SIR CLAUDE

                  I'm not laughing.
So what you wanted was to inspire an artist!

LADY ELIZABETH

Or to inspire a poet. I thought Tony was a poet.
Because he wrote me poems. And he was so beautiful.
I know now that poets don't look like poets:
And financiers, it seems, don't look like potters —
Is that what I mean? I'm getting confused.
I thought I was escaping from a world that I loathed
In Tony — and then, too late, I discovered
He belonged to the world I wanted to escape from.
He was so commonplace! I wanted to forget him,

And so, I suppose, I wanted to forget
Colby. But Colby is an artist.

SIR CLAUDE

A musician.
I am a disappointed craftsman,
And Colby is a disappointed composer.
I should have been a second-rate potter,
And he would have been a second-rate organist.
We have both chosen . . . obedience to the facts.

LADY ELIZABETH

I believe that was what *I* was trying to do.
It's very strange, Claude, but this is the first time
I have talked to you, without feeling very stupid.
You always made me feel that I wasn't worth talking to.

SIR CLAUDE

And you always made me feel that *your* interests
Were much too deep for discussion with *me*:
Health cures. And modern art — so long as it was modern —
And dervish dancing.

LADY ELIZABETH

Dervish dancing!
Really, Claude, how absurd you are!
Not that there isn't a lot to be learnt,
I don't doubt, from the dervish rituals.
But it doesn't matter what Mrs. Guzzard tells us,
If it satisfies Colby. Whatever happens
He shall be *our* son.
[*A knock on the door. Enter* EGGERSON]

SIR CLAUDE

Good morning, Eggerson.

EGGERSON

Good morning, Sir Claude. And Lady
Elizabeth!

SIR CLAUDE

I'm sorry, Eggerson, to bring you up to London
At such short notice.

EGGERSON

                    Don't say that, Sir Claude.
It's true, I haven't much nowadays to bring me;
But Mrs. E. wishes I'd come up oftener!
Isn't that like the ladies! She used to complain
At my being up in London five or six days a week:
But now she says: 'You're becoming such a countryman!
You're losing touch with public affairs.'
The fact is, she misses the contact with London,
Though she doesn't admit it. She misses my news
When I came home in the evening. And the late editions
Of the papers that I picked up at Liverpool Street.
But I've so much to do, in Joshua Park —
Apart from the garden — that I've not an idle moment.
And really, now, I'm quite lost in London.
Every time I come, I notice the traffic
Has got so much worse.

SIR CLAUDE

                    Yes, it's always getting worse.

LADY ELIZABETH

— I hope Mrs. Eggerson is well?

EGGERSON

                        Pretty well.
She's always low-spirited, around this season,
When we're getting near the anniversary.

SIR CLAUDE

The anniversary? Of your son's death?

EGGERSON

Of the day we got the news. We don't often speak of it;

Yet I know what's on her mind, for days beforehand.
But here I am, talking about ourselves!
And we've more important business, I imagine.

SIR CLAUDE

Eggerson, I'm expecting Mrs. Guzzard.

EGGERSON

Indeed! Mrs. Guzzard! And why are we expecting her?

SIR CLAUDE

I have asked her to come. Lady Elizabeth
Is sure that she knows the name of Mrs. Guzzard.

LADY ELIZABETH

Mrs. Guzzard, of Teddington.

EGGERSON

            Ah, indeed!
I shouldn't have expected her name to be known to you.

SIR CLAUDE

She'd been questioning Colby about himself,
And he mentioned the name of his aunt, Mrs. Guzzard.
Now she's convinced that Mrs. Guzzard
Of Teddington is the name of the person
To whom her own child was entrusted.

EGGERSON

What an amazing coincidence!

SIR CLAUDE

            That's what it is,
Unless she is mistaken . . .

LADY ELIZABETH
            Now, Claude!

SIR CLAUDE

And she came to the conclusion that her child must be Colby,
So I told her the truth. But she cannot believe it.

LADY ELIZABETH

Claude, that's not quite right. Let me explain.
I am convinced that Sir Claude is mistaken,
Or has been deceived, and that Colby is my son.
I feel sure he is. But I don't want to know:
I am perfectly content to leave things as they are,
So that we may regard him as *our* son.

SIR CLAUDE

That is perfectly correct. It is Colby
Who is not satisfied with that solution.
He insists upon the facts. And that is why
I have asked Mrs. Guzzard here. *She* doesn't know that.

EGGERSON

A natural line for Mr. Simpkins to take,
If I may say so. Of course, we might discover
Another Mrs. Guzzard . . .

LADY ELIZABETH
Two Mrs. Guzzards?

EGGERSON

I agree, it is a most uncommon name,
But stranger things have happened.

LADY ELIZABETH
And both in Teddington

EGGERSON

I agree, that would be most surprising.
And at the same address

LADY ELIZABETH
I don't know the address.

Mrs. Guzzard of Teddington, that's all I know,
And that I could swear to.

EGGERSON

                    It does seem unlikely
That there should be two Mrs. Guzzards in Teddington.
But assuming, for the moment, only one Mrs. Guzzard,
Could there not have been two babies?

LADY ELIZABETH

Two babies, Eggerson?

EGGERSON

                    I was only suggesting
That perhaps Mrs. Guzzard made a profession
Of . . . looking after other people's children?
In a manner of speaking, it's perfectly respectable.

SIR CLAUDE

You're suggesting that she ran a baby farm.
That's most unlikely, nowadays.
Besides, I should have noticed it. I visited her house
Often. I never saw more than one baby.

EGGERSON

She might have taken in another one
As a temporary accommodation —
On suitable terms. But if she did that,
We must enquire what became of the other one.

SIR CLAUDE

But *this* baby was Colby.

LADY ELIZABETH

                    Of course it was Colby.

SIR CLAUDE

But Eggerson, you really can't ask me to believe
That she took two babies, and got them mixed.

LADY ELIZABETH

That seems to be what happened. And now we must find
    out
What became of your child, Claude.

SIR CLAUDE

                    What became of *my*
child!
The mother of *my* child was Mrs. Guzzard's sister.
She wouldn't dispose of *him*. It's your child, Elizabeth,
Whom we must try to trace.

EGGERSON

                    If there was another child
Then we must try to trace it. Certainly, Sir Claude:
Our first step must be to question Mrs. Guzzard.

SIR CLAUDE

And that's what we are here for. She will be here shortly.
And when she arrives I will summon Colby.
I wanted you here first, to explain the situation:
And I thought I would like you to conduct the proceedings.
Will you sit at the desk?

EGGERSON

                    If you wish, Sir Claude.
I do feel more at ease when I'm behind a desk:
It's second nature.

SIR CLAUDE

                    And put the case to her.
Don't let her think that *I* have any doubts:
You are putting the questions on behalf of my wife.

EGGERSON

I understand, Sir Claude: I understand completely.

[*A knock on the door*]

SIR CLAUDE

Good Lord, she's here already! Well . . . Come in!
[*Enter* LUCASTA]

LUCASTA

Is this a meeting? I came to speak to Colby.
I'm sorry.

SIR CLAUDE

    Colby will be here.
But you're not involved in this meeting, Lucasta.
Won't it do another time?

LUCASTA

            I came to apologise
To Colby. No matter. It'll do another time.
Oh, I'm glad you're here, Eggy! You're such a support.
In any case, I've an announcement to make,
And I might as well make it now. If you'll listen.

SIR CLAUDE

Of course I'll listen. But we haven't much time.

LUCASTA

It won't take much time. I'm going to marry B.

SIR CLAUDE

To marry B.! But I thought that was all settled.

LUCASTA

Yes, of course, Claude. You thought everything settled.
That was just the trouble. You made it so obvious
That this would be the ideal solution
From your point of view. To get me off your hands.
Oh, I know what a nuisance you've always found me!
And I haven't made it easier. I didn't try to.
And knowing that you wanted me to marry B.
Made me determined that I wouldn't. Just to spite you,

92

I dare say. That was why I took an interest
In Colby. Because you thought he was too good for me.

SIR CLAUDE

In Colby!

LUCASTA

Why not? That's perfectly natural.
But I'm grateful to Colby. But for Colby
I'd never have come to appreciate B.

SIR CLAUDE

But Colby! Lucasta, if I'd suspected this
I would have explained. Colby is your brother.

EGGERSON

Half-brother, Miss Angel.

SIR CLAUDE

Yes, half-brother.

LUCASTA

What do you mean?

SIR CLAUDE

Colby is my son.

LADY ELIZABETH

That is what Sir Claude believes. Claude, let me explain.

SIR CLAUDE

No, I'll explain. There's been some misunderstanding.
My wife believes that Colby is *her* son.
That is the reason for this meeting today.
We're awaiting Mrs. Guzzard — Colby's aunt.

LUCASTA

Colby's aunt? You make my brain reel.

SIR CLAUDE

I ought to have made things clear to you
At the time when he came here. But I didn't trust you
To keep a secret. There were reasons for that
Which no longer exist. But I ought to have told you.

LUCASTA

Well, I don't understand. What I do understand
Is Colby's behaviour. If he knew it.

SIR CLAUDE

                          He knew it.

LUCASTA

Why didn't he tell me? Perhaps he was about to.
Anyway, I *knew* there had been some mistake.
You don't know at all what I'm talking about!
But if he knew that he was your son
He must have been staggered when I said I was your daugh-
    ter!
I came to thank him for the shock he'd given me.
He made me see what I really wanted.
B. makes me feel safe. And that's what I want.
And somehow or other, I've something to give him —
Something that he needs. Colby doesn't need me,
He doesn't need anyone. He's fascinating,
But he's undependable. He has his own world,
And he might vanish into it at any moment —
At just the moment when you needed him most!
And he doesn't depend upon other people, either.
B. needs me. He's been hurt by life, just as I have,
And we can help each other. Oh, I know you think of him
Simply as a business man. As you thought of me
Simply as a nuisance. We're suited to each other:
You thought so too, Claude, but for the wrong reasons,
And that put me off. So I'm grateful to Colby.

SIR CLAUDE

I don't know what's happened, but nevertheless
I'm sure that you have made the right decision.

LUCASTA

But the reasons why you think so are the wrong ones.

LADY ELIZABETH

And I'm sure too, Lucasta, you have made a wise decision.

LUCASTA

And I know very well why *you* think so:
You think we're suited because we're both common.
B. knows you think him common. And so he pretends
To be very common, because he knows you think so.
You gave us our parts. And we've shown that we can play
    them.

LADY ELIZABETH

I don't think you ought to say that, Lucasta;
I have always been a person of liberal views —
That's why I never got on with my family.

LUCASTA

Well, I'm not a person of liberal views.
I'm very conventional. And I'm not ashamed of it.

SIR CLAUDE

Perhaps you are right. I'm not sure of anything.
Perhaps, as you say, I've misunderstood B.,
And I've never thought that I understood *you*;
And I certainly fail to understand Colby.

LADY ELIZABETH

But you and I, Claude, can understand each other,
No matter how late. And perhaps that will help us
To understand other people. I hope so.
Lucasta, I regard you as a . . . step-daughter;
And shall be happy to accept Mr. Kaghan as a son-in-law.

LUCASTA

Thank you. I'm sure he'll appreciate *that*.
But that reminds me. He's waiting downstairs.
I don't suppose you want *us* at your meeting.

EGGERSON

Allow me. May I make a suggestion?
Though first of all I must take the occasion
To wish Miss Angel every happiness.
And I'm sure she will be happy. Mr. Kaghan
Is one of the most promising young men in the City,
And he has a heart of gold. So have you, Miss Angel.
We have this very important interview,
But I'm sure that we want to greet the happy pair.
It's all in the family. Why not let them wait downstairs
And come back after Mrs. Guzzard has left?

SIR CLAUDE

That's not a bad idea. If Colby agrees.

LUCASTA

I trust you, Eggy. And I want to make my peace with him.

SIR CLAUDE

We'll get him now.
                    [*reaches for the telephone*]
[*A knock. Enter* COLBY]

COLBY

                    Have I come too soon?
I'm afraid I got impatient of waiting.

LUCASTA

Colby! I've not come to interrupt your meeting.
I've been told what it's about. But I did come to see you.
I came to apologise for my behaviour
The other afternoon.

96

COLBY
Apologise?

SIR CLAUDE
I've told her.

COLBY
But why should you apologise?

LUCASTA
Oh, because I knew
That I must have misunderstood your reaction.
It wouldn't have been like you — the way I thought it was.
You're much too . . . detached, ever to be shocked
In the way I thought you were. I was ashamed
Of what I was telling you, and so I was expecting
What I thought I got. But I couldn't believe it!
It isn't like you, to despise people:
You don't care enough.

COLBY
I don't care enough?

LUCASTA
No. You're either above caring,
Or else you're insensible — I don't mean insensitive!
But you're terribly cold. Or else you've some fire
To warm you, that isn't the same kind of fire
That warms other people. You're either an egotist
Or something so different from the rest of us
That we can't judge you. That's you, Colby.

COLBY
That's me, is it? I simply don't know.
Perhaps you know me better than I know myself.
But now you know what I am . . .

LUCASTA
Who you are,

97   E.C.C.

In the sense I've been told that you're my brother;
Which makes it more difficult to know *what* you are.
It may be there's no one so hard to understand
As one's brother . . .

COLBY

Or sister . . .

LUCASTA

What's so difficult
Is to recognise the limits of one's understanding.
It may be that understanding, as a brother and a sister,
Will come, in time. Perhaps, one day
We may understand each other. And accept the fact
That we're not necessary to each other
In the way we might have been. But a different way
That reveals itself in time. And perhaps — who knows? —
We might become more necessary to each other,
As a brother and a sister, than we could have been
In any other form of relationship.

COLBY

I want you to be happy.

LUCASTA

I shall be happy,
If you will accept me as a sister
For the happiness that relationship may bring us
In twenty or thirty or forty years' time.
I shall be happy. I'm going to marry B.
I know you like B.

COLBY

I'm very fond of him;
And I'm glad to think he'll be my brother-in-law.
I shall need you, both of you, Lucasta!

LUCASTA

We'll mean something to you. But you don't *need* anybody.

EGGERSON

And now may I interrupt, Miss Angel?
Why shouldn't you and Mr. Kaghan wait downstairs
And rejoin us when this interview is over?
I'm sure Mr. Simpkins will concur in this proposal.

COLBY

Of course I'd like them . . . Can't B. come up now?

EGGERSON

Better wait till afterwards.

SIR CLAUDE

Quite right, Eggerson.

LUCASTA

Good-bye, Colby.

COLBY

Why do you say good-bye?

LUCASTA

Good-bye to Colby as Lucasta knew him,
And good-bye to the Lucasta whom Colby knew.
We've changed since then: as you said, we're always
        changing.
When I come back, we'll be brother and sister —
Or so I hope. Yes, in any event,
Good-bye, Colby.

[*Exit* LUCASTA]

COLBY

Good-bye then, Lucasta.

EGGERSON

And now, how soon are we expecting Mrs. Guzzard?

99

SIR CLAUDE

[*looking at his watch*]

She ought to be here now! It's surprising,
I hadn't been aware how the time was passing,
What with Lucasta's unexpected visit.
She ought to be here. It wouldn't be like her
To be late for an appointment. She always mentioned it
If *I* was late when I went to see her.
[*Enter* LUCASTA]

LUCASTA

I'm sorry to come back. It's an anti-climax.
But there seems to be nobody to answer the door.
I've just let someone in. It's the Mrs. Guzzard
Whom you are expecting. She looks rather formidable.

SIR CLAUDE

It's Parkman's day off. But where's the parlourmaid?

LUCASTA

I thought I heard someone singing in the pantry.

LADY ELIZABETH

Oh, I forgot. It's Gertrude's quiet hour.
I've been giving her lessons in recollection.
But she shouldn't be singing.

LUCASTA

Well, what shall I do?

EGGERSON

Let me go down and explain to Mrs. Guzzard
and then bring her up.

SIR CLAUDE

No, I want you here, Eggerson.
Will you show her up, Lucasta?

LUCASTA

I'll make B. do it.

[*Exit* LUCASTA]

SIR CLAUDE

I wish you could arrange the servants' time-table better.
This is a most unfortunate beginning.

LADY ELIZABETH

She's been making progress, under my direction;
But she shouldn't have been singing.

SIR CLAUDE

Well, are we ready?

[*A quiet knock. Enter* KAGHAN, *escorting* MRS. GUZZARD.
    Exit KAGHAN]
Good morning, Mrs. Guzzard. I must apologise:
I'm afraid there has been some domestic incompetence.
You should have been announced.

MRS. GUZZARD

I believe I was punctual.
But I didn't mind waiting in the least, Sir Claude.
I know that you are always much engaged.

SIR CLAUDE

First, let me introduce you to my wife.
Lady Elizabeth Mulhammer.

LADY ELIZABETH

Good morning, Mrs. Guzzard.
You don't know me, but I know about you:
We have more in common than you are aware of.

MRS. GUZZARD

I suppose you mean Colby?

LADY ELIZABETH

Yes. To do with Colby.

SIR CLAUDE

Elizabeth, you know we are to leave that to Eggerson.
This is Mr. Eggerson, Mrs. Guzzard:
My confidential clerk. That is to say,
Colby's predecessor, who recently retired.
Now he lives . . . in the country. But he knows the whole
          story:
He's been in my confidence — and I may say, my friend —
For very many years. So I asked him to be present.
I hope you don't mind?

MRS. GUZZARD

Why should I mind?
I have heard about Mr. Eggerson from Colby.
I am very happy to make his acquaintance.

SIR CLAUDE

And I thought he might . . . conduct the proceedings:
He's the very soul of tact and discretion.

MRS. GUZZARD

Certainly, Sir Claude, if that is what you wish.
But is the subject of this meeting —
I suppose to do with Colby — so very confidential?

EGGERSON

Yes, that is what I should call it, Mrs. Guzzard.
I take it, Sir Claude, I should open the discussion?

SIR CLAUDE

If you please, Eggerson.

EGGERSON

Then let's make a start.
The question has to do, as you surmised, with Mr. Simpkins.
It also concerns a problem of paternity.

LADY ELIZABETH

Or of maternity.

SIR CLAUDE

Don't interrupt, Elizabeth.

MRS. GUZZARD

I don't understand you.

EGGERSON

It's this way, Mrs. Guzzard.
It is only recently that Lady Elizabeth
Heard your name mentioned, by Mr. Simpkins.
She was struck by your name and your living in Teddington.
And now we must go back, many years:
Well, not so many years — when you get to my age
The past and the future both seem very brief —
But long enough ago for the question to be possible.
Lady Elizabeth, before her marriage
Had a child . . .

LADY ELIZABETH

A son.

EGGERSON

Had a son
Whom she could not, in the circumstances, acknowledge.
That happens not infrequently, Mrs. Guzzard.

MRS. GUZZARD

So I am aware. I have known it to happen.

EGGERSON

— Who was taken charge of by the father.
That is to say, placed out to be cared for
Till further notice by a foster-mother.
Unfortunately, the father died suddenly . . .

LADY ELIZABETH

He was run over. By a rhinoceros
In Tanganyika.

SIR CLAUDE

That's not relevant.
Leave it to Eggerson.

EGGERSON

The father died abroad.
Lady Elizabeth did not know the name of the lady
Who had taken the child. Or rather, had forgotten it.
She was not, in any case, in a position
In which she could have instituted enquiries.
So, for many years, she has been without a clue
Until the other day. This son, Mrs. Guzzard,
If he is alive, must be a grown man.
I believe you have had no children of your own;
But I'm sure you can sympathise.

MRS. GUZZARD

I can sympathise.
I had a child, and lost him Not in the way
That Lady Elizabeth's child was lost.
Let us hope that her son may be restored to her.

EGGERSON

That is exactly what we are aiming at.
We have a clue — or what appears to be a clue.
That is why Sir Claude has asked you to be present.

MRS. GUZZARD

You think I might be able to help you?

EGGERSON

It seems just possible. A few days ago,
As I said, Lady Elizabeth learned your name;
And the name struck her as being familiar.

MRS. GUZZARD

Indeed? It is not a very common name.

EGGERSON

That is what impressed her. Mrs. Guzzard
Of Teddington! Lady Elizabeth is convinced
That it was a Mrs. Guzzard of Teddington
To whom her new-born child was confided.
Of course she might be mistaken about Teddington . . .

LADY ELIZABETH

I am *not* mistaken about Teddington.

EGGERSON

I am only suggesting, Lady Elizabeth,
There are other places that sound like Teddington
But not so many names that sound like Guzzard —
Or if there are, they are equally uncommon.
But, Mrs. Guzzard, this is where you can help us —
Do you know of any other Mrs. Guzzard?

MRS. GUZZARD

                                        None.

EGGERSON

Whether, I mean, in Teddington or elsewhere?
Now I must ask a more delicate question:
Did you, at any time, take in a child —
A child, that is, of parents unknown to you —
Under such conditions?

MRS. GUZZARD

                Yes, I did take in a child.
My husband and I were childless . . . at the time,
And very poor. It offered two advantages.

EGGERSON

And did you know the name of the father
Or of the mother?

105

MRS. GUZZARD

I was not told either.
I understood the child was very well connected:
Otherwise, I should not have taken him.
But he was brought to me by a third party,
Through whom the monthly payments were made.

EGGERSON

The terms were satisfactory?

MRS. GUZZARD

Very satisfactory —
So long, that is to say, as the money was forthcoming.

EGGERSON

Did the payments come to an end?

MRS. GUZZARD

Very suddenly.

LADY ELIZABETH

That must have been when Tony met with his accident.

MRS. GUZZARD

I was informed that the father had died
Without making a will.

LADY ELIZABETH

He was very careless.

MRS. GUZZARD

And that the heirs acknowledged no responsibility.
The mother, I suppose, could have got an order
If she could have established the paternity;
But I didn't know who she was! What could I do?

LADY ELIZABETH

Oh, Claude, you see? You understand, Colby?

SIR CLAUDE
Don't be certain yet, Elizabeth.

LADY ELIZABETH
There is no doubt about it.
Colby is my son.

MRS. GUZZARD
Your son, Lady Elizabeth?
Are you suggesting that I kept a child of yours
And deceived Sir Claude by pretending it was his?

SIR CLAUDE
That is just the point. My wife has convinced herself
That Colby is her son. I know he is *my* son.
And I asked you here so that you might tell her so.

EGGERSON
Don't take this as a personal reflection,
Mrs. Guzzard. Far from it. You must make allowances
For a mother who has been hoping against hope
To find her son. Put yourself in her position.
If you had lost your son, in a similar way,
Wouldn't you grasp at any straw
That offered hope of finding him?

MRS. GUZZARD
Perhaps I should.

LADY ELIZABETH
There isn't a shadow of doubt in my mind.
I'm surprised that you, Eggerson, with your legal training,
Should talk about straws! Colby is my son.

MRS. GUZZARD
In the circumstances, I ignore that remark.

EGGERSON
May I pour a drop of oil on these troubled waters?

107

Let us approach the question from another angle,
And ask Mrs. Guzzard what became of the child
She took in, which may have been Lady Elizabeth's.

Sir Claude

That's a very sensible suggestion, Eggerson.
A breath of sanity. Thank you for that.

Mrs. Guzzard

We parted with it. A dear little boy.
I was happy to have him while the payments were made;
But we could not afford to adopt the child,
Or continue to keep him, when the payments ended.

Eggerson

And how did you dispose of him?

Mrs. Guzzard

We had neighbours
Who were childless, and eager to adopt a child.
They had taken a fancy to him. So they adopted him.
Then they left Teddington, and we lost sight of them.

Eggerson

But you know their name?

Mrs. Guzzard

Yes, I know their name:
Like mine, a somewhat unusual one.
Perhaps it might be possible to trace them.
The name was Kaghan.

Sir Claude

Their name was Kaghan!

Mrs. Guzzard

K-A-G-H-A-N. An odd name.
They were excellent people. Nonconformists.

EGGERSON

And the child, I suppose he had a Christian name?

MRS. GUZZARD

There was nothing to show that the child had been baptised
When it came to us; but we could not be sure.
My husband was particular in such matters,
So we had it given conditional baptism.

EGGERSON

What name did you give him?

MRS. GUZZARD

We named the child Barnabas.

LADY ELIZABETH

Barnabas? There's never been such a name
In my family. Or, I'm sure, in his father's.
But how did he come to be called Colby?

SIR CLAUDE

But, Elizabeth, it isn't Colby!
Don't you see who it is?

MRS. GUZZARD

My husband chose the name.
We had been married in the church of St. Barnabas.

COLBY

Barnabas Kaghan. Is he the little cousin
Who died? Don't you remember, Aunt Sarah,
My finding a rattle and a jingle-bell,
And your telling me I had had a little cousin
Who had died?

MRS. GUZZARD

Yes, Colby, that is what I told you.

109

LADY ELIZABETH

So my child is living. I was sure of that.
But I believe that Colby is Barnabas.

SIR CLAUDE

No, Elizabeth, Barnabas is Barnabas.
I must explain this, Mrs. Guzzard.
I have a very promising young colleague —
In fact, the young man who showed you upstairs —
Whose name is Barnabas Kaghan.

LADY ELIZABETH

Barnabas?

SIR CLAUDE

Yes, Elizabeth. He sometimes has to sign his full name.
But he doesn't like the name, for some reason;
So we call him B.

MRS. GUZZARD

A very good name.
He ought to be proud of it.

LADY ELIZABETH

How old is this Barnabas?

SIR CLAUDE

About twenty-eight, I think.

MRS. GUZZARD

He should be twenty-eight.

LADY ELIZABETH

Then I must be out in my calculations.

SIR CLAUDE

That wouldn't surprise me.

LADY ELIZABETH

Yes, what year was it?
I'm getting so confused. What with Colby being Barnabas —
I mean, not Barnabas. And Mr. Kaghan
Being Barnabas. I suppose I'll get used to it.

COLBY

But he's waiting downstairs! Isn't this the moment
For me to bring him up? And Lucasta?

EGGERSON

An excellent suggestion, Mr. Simpkins.

[*Exit* COLBY]

EGGERSON

And now, if you agree, Lady Elizabeth,
We can ask Mr. Kaghan about his parents;
And if Mr. and Mrs. Kaghan are still living
Mrs. Guzzard should be able to identify them.

LADY ELIZABETH

And will that prove that Mr. Kaghan —
This Mr. Kaghan — is my son?

EGGERSON

It creates an inherent probability —
If that's the right expression.

SIR CLAUDE

I believe, Elizabeth,
That you have found your son.

EGGERSON

Subject to confirmation.

LADY ELIZABETH

And to my being able to adjust myself to it.
[*Re-enter* COLBY, *with* KAGHAN *and* LUCASTA]

111

COLBY

I have told them to be prepared for a surprise.

LADY ELIZABETH

Barnabas! Is your name Barnabas?

KAGHAN

Why, yes, it is. Did you tell her, Sir Claude?

SIR CLAUDE

No, B. It was Mrs. Guzzard who revealed it.
This is Mr. Barnabas Kaghan —
Mrs. Guzzard. And . . . my daughter Lucasta.

KAGHAN

But how did Mrs. Guzzard know my name?

MRS. GUZZARD

Were Mr. and Mrs. Alfred Kaghan your parents?

KAGHAN

Yes. They are. My adoptive parents.

MRS. GUZZARD

And did they at one time live in Teddington?

KAGHAN

I believe they did. But why are you interested?

MRS. GUZZARD

Lady Elizabeth, I believe that this is your son.
If so, I am cleared from your unjust suspicion.

EGGERSON

Mr. Kaghan, are your adoptive parents living?

KAGHAN

In Kent. They wanted to retire to the country.

So I found them a little place near Sevenoaks
Where they keep bees. But why are you asking?

LADY ELIZABETH

Because, Barnabas, it seems you are my son.

EGGERSON

You will wish to obtain confirmation
Of this interesting discovery, Mr. Kaghan,
By putting your adoptive parents in touch
With Mrs. Guzzard. It's for them to confirm
That they took you, as a child, from Mrs. Guzzard,
To whom, it seems, you had first been entrusted.

KAGHAN

I really don't know what emotion to register . . .

LUCASTA

You don't need to talk that language any longer:
Just say you're embarrassed.

KAGHAN

                    Well, I am embarrassed.
If Lady Elizabeth is my mother . . .

LADY ELIZABETH

There is no doubt whatever about it, Barnabas.
I am your mother.

KAGHAN

              But who was my father?

LADY ELIZABETH

He died very suddenly. Of a fatal accident
When you were very young. That is why you were adopted.

KAGHAN

But what did he do? Was he a financier?

LADY ELIZABETH

He was not good at figures. Your business ability
Comes, I suppose, from my side of the family.
But he was in a very good regiment —
For a time, at least.

KAGHAN

Well, I must get used to that.
But I should like to know how I ought to address you,
Lady Elizabeth. I've always been accustomed
To regard Mrs. Kaghan as my mother.

LADY ELIZABETH

Then in order to avoid any danger of confusion
You may address me as Aunt Elizabeth.

KAGHAN

That's easier, certainly.

LADY ELIZABETH

And I shall wish to meet them.
Claude, we must invite the Kaghans to dinner.

SIR CLAUDE

By all means, Elizabeth.

KAGHAN

But, Lady Elizabeth —
I mean, Aunt Elizabeth: if I call you Aunt Elizabeth
Would you mind very much calling me . . . just 'B'?

LADY ELIZABETH

Certainly, if you prefer that, Barnabas.

LUCASTA

Why is it that you don't like the name of Barnabas?

KAGHAN

I don't want people calling me 'Barney' —

Barney Kaghan! Kaghan's all right.
But Barney Kaghan — it sounds rather flashy:
It wouldn't make the right impression in the City.

LUCASTA

When you're an alderman, you'll be Sir Barney Kaghan!

LADY ELIZABETH

And I'm very glad you're announcing your engagement.
Lucasta, I shall take charge of your wedding.

LUCASTA

We'd meant to be married very quietly
In a register office.

LADY ELIZABETH

You must have a church wedding.

MRS. GUZZARD

I am glad to hear you say so, Lady Elizabeth.
But are *you* satisfied?

LADY ELIZABETH

Satisfied? What about?

MRS. GUZZARD

That your suspicions of me were wholly unfounded.

LADY ELIZABETH

Oh, Mrs. Guzzard, I had no suspicions!
I thought there had been a confusion — that's all.

MRS. GUZZARD

I feared there might be a confusion in your mind
Between the meaning of *confusion* and *imposture*.

SIR CLAUDE

I don't think there is any confusion now:

I'm sure that my wife is perfectly convinced;
And Mr. Kaghan's . . . mother, I am sure, will confirm it.

MRS. GUZZARD

That is as much to my interest as anyone's.
But will your wife be satisfied,
When she has the evidence the Kaghans will supply,
To recognise Barnabas Kaghan as her son?
                    [to LADY ELIZABETH]
Are you contented to have him as your son?

SIR CLAUDE

That seems a strange question, Mrs. Guzzard.

MRS. GUZZARD

I have been asked here to answer strange questions —
And now it is my turn to ask them.
I should like to gratify everyone's wishes.

LADY ELIZABETH

Oh, of course . . . Yes, I'm sure . . . I shall be very happy.

MRS. GUZZARD

You wished for your son, and now you have your son.
We all of us have to adapt ourselves
To the wish that is granted. That can be a painful process,
As I know. And you, Barnabas Kaghan,
Are you satisfied to find yourself the son
Of Lady Elizabeth Mulhammer?

KAGHAN

It's very much better than being a foundling —
If I can live up to it. And . . . yes, of course,
If I can make it right with my parents.
I'm fond of them, you know.

LADY ELIZABETH

                    I shall see to that, Barnabas.

116

B. — if you don't mind, Aunt Elizabeth.

LADY ELIZABETH

B. — and I'm sure we shall become great friends.

EGGERSON

I'm sure we all wish for nothing better.

MRS. GUZZARD

Wishes, when realised, sometimes turn
Against those who have made them.
   [*to* LADY ELIZABETH *and* KAGHAN]
         Not, I think, with you.
    [*to* LUCASTA]
Nor, so far as I can judge, with you.
Perhaps you are the wisest wisher here:
I shall not ask you whether you are satisfied
To be the wife of Barnabas Kaghan,
The daughter-in-law of Lady Elizabeth,
And the daughter of Sir Claude Mulhammer.

SIR CLAUDE

That is *my* concern — that she shall be satisfied
To be my daughter.

MRS. GUZZARD

    Now, Colby,
I must ask *you* now, have you had your wish?

SIR CLAUDE

Colby only wanted to be sure of the truth.

COLBY

That is a very strange question, Aunt Sarah:
To which I can only give a strange answer.
Sir Claude is right: I wished to know the truth.
What it is, doesn't matter. All I wanted was relief

117

From the nagging annoyance of knowing there's a fact
That one doesn't know. But the fact itself
Is unimportant, once one knows it.

MRS. GUZZARD

You had no preference? Between a father and a mother?

COLBY

I've never had a father or a mother —
It's different for B. He's had his foster-parents,
So he can afford another relationship.
Let my mother rest in peace. As for my father —
I have the idea of a father.
It's only just come to me. I should like a father
Whom I had never known and couldn't know now,
Because he would have died before I was born
Or before I could remember; whom I could get to know
Only by report, by documents —
The story of his life, of his success or failure . . .
Perhaps his failure more than his success —
By objects that belonged to him, and faded photographs
In which I should try to decipher a likeness;
Whose image I could create in my own mind,
To live with that image. An ordinary man
Whose life I could in some way perpetuate
By being the person he would have liked to be,
And by doing the things he had wanted to do.

MRS. GUZZARD

Whose son would you wish to be, Colby:
Sir Claude's — or the son of some other man
Obscure and silent? A dead man, Colby.
Be careful what you say.

COLBY

            A dead obscure man.

MRS. GUZZARD

You shall have your wish. And when you have your wish
118

You will have to come to terms with it. You shall have a
 father
Dead, and unknown to you.

SIR CLAUDE

What do you mean?

MRS. GUZZARD

Colby is not your son, Sir Claude.

COLBY

Who was my father, then?

MRS. GUZZARD

Herbert Guzzard.
You are the son of a disappointed musician.

COLBY

And who was my mother?

MRS. GUZZARD

Let your mother rest in peace.
I *was* your mother; but I chose to be your aunt.
So you may have your wish, and have no mother.

SIR CLAUDE

Mrs. Guzzard, this is perfectly incredible!
You couldn't have carried out such a deception
Over all these years. And why *should* you have deceived me?

EGGERSON

Mrs. Guzzard, can you substantiate this statement?

MRS. GUZZARD

Registration of birth. To Herbert and Sarah Guzzard
A son.

EGGERSON

And what about your sister and her child?

MRS. GUZZARD

Registration of death. The child was never born.

SIR CLAUDE

I don't believe it. I simply can't believe it.
Mrs. Guzzard, you are inventing this fiction
In response to what Colby said he wanted.

EGGERSON

I'll examine the records myself, Sir Claude.
Not that we doubt your word, Mrs. Guzzard:
But in a matter of such extreme importance
You'll understand the need for exact confirmation.

MRS. GUZZARD

I understand that, Mr. Eggerson. Quite well.

SIR CLAUDE

I shall not believe it. I'll not believe those records.
You pretend to have carried out a deception
For twenty-five years? It's quite impossible.

MRS. GUZZARD

I had no intention of deceiving you, Sir Claude,
Till you deceived yourself. When you went to Canada
My sister found that she was to have a child:
That much is true. I also was expecting one.
That you did not know. It did not concern you.
As I have just said, my sister died
Before the child could be born. You were very far away;
I sent you a message, which never reached you.
On your return, you came at once to see me;
And I found that I had to break the news to you.
You saw the child. You assumed that it was yours;
And you were so pleased, I shrank, at the moment,
From undeceiving you. And then I thought — why not?
My husband also had died. I was left very poor.
If I let you continue to think the child was yours,

My son was assured of a proper start in life —
That I knew. And it would make you so happy!
If I said the child was mine, what future could he have?
And then I was frightened by what I had done.
Though I had never said 'this child is yours',
I feared you would ask for the birth certificate.
You never did. And so it went on.

SIR CLAUDE

This is horribly plausible. But it can't be true.

MRS. GUZZARD

Consider, Sir Claude. Would I tell you all this
Unless it was true? In telling you the truth
I am sacrificing my ambitions for Colby.
I am sacrificing also my previous sacrifice.
This is even greater than the sacrifice I made
When I let you claim him. Do you think it is a small thing
For me, to see my life's ambition come to nothing?
When I gave up my place as Colby's mother
I gave up something I could never have back.
Don't you understand that this revelation
Drives the knife deeper and twists it in the wound?
I had very much rather that the facts were otherwise.

COLBY

I believe you. I must believe you:
This gives me freedom.

SIR CLAUDE
But, Colby —

If this should be true — of course it can't be true! —
But I see you believe it. You want to believe it.
Well, believe it, then. But don't let it make a difference
To our relations. Or, perhaps, for the better?
Perhaps we'll be happier together if you think
I am not your father. I'll accept that.
If you will stay with me. It shall make no difference
To my plans for your future.

COLBY

Thank you, Sir Claude.
You're a very generous man. But now I know who was my
    father
I must follow my father — so that I may come to know him.

SIR CLAUDE

What do you mean?

COLBY

I want to be an organist.
It doesn't matter about success —
I aimed too high before — beyond my capacity.
I thought I didn't want to be an organist
When I found I had no chance of getting to the top —
That is, to become the organist of a cathedral.
But my father was an unsuccessful organist.

MRS. GUZZARD

You should say, Colby, not very successful.

COLBY

And I wish to follow my father.

SIR CLAUDE

But, Colby:
Don't you remember the talk we had —
So very long ago! — when we shared our ambitions
And shared our disappointment. And you described your
    feelings
On beginning to learn the ways of business;
The exhilaration of finding you could handle
Matters you would have thought so uncongenial;
And the way in which you felt that you were changing?
That conversation would have convinvced me
With no other evidence, that you were my son,
Because you described my own experience, exactly.
Does that mean nothing to you, the experience we shared?

122

Heaven knows — and you know — I put no obstruction
In the way of your fulfilling your musical ambitions —
Had you been able to fulfil them.
Believe, if you like, that I am not your father:
I'll accept that. I put no claim upon you —
Except the claim of our likeness to each other.
We have undergone the same disillusionment:
I want us to make the best of it, together.

COLBY

No, Sir Claude. I hate to hurt you
As I am hurting you. But it is very different.
As long as I believed that you were my father
I was content to have had the same ambitions
And in the same way to accept their failure.
You had your father before you, as a model;
You knew your inheritance. Now I know mine.

SIR CLAUDE

I shall never ask you to think of me as a father;
All I ask you is — to regard me as a friend.

COLBY

But you would still think of me as your son.
There can be no relation of father and son
Unless it works both ways. For you to regard me —
As you would — as your son, when I could not think of you
As my father: if I accepted that
I should be guilty towards you. I like you too much.
You've become a man without illusions
About himself, and without ambitions.
Now that I've abandoned *my* illusions and ambitions
All that's left is love. But not on false pretences:
That's why I must leave you.

SIR CLAUDE
Eggerson!

Can't you persuade him?

LADY ELIZABETH

Yes. My poor Claude!
Do try to help him, Eggerson.

EGGERSON

I wouldn't venture.
Mr. Simpkins is a man who knows his own mind.
Is it true, Mr. Simpkins, that what you desire
Is to become the organist of some parish church?

COLBY

That is what I want. If anyone will take me.

EGGERSON

If so, I happen to know of a vacancy
In my own parish, in Joshua Park —
If it should appeal to you. The organist we had
Died two months ago. We've been looking for another.

COLBY

Do you think that they would give me a trial?

EGGERSON

Give you a trial? I'm certain.
Good organists don't seem to want to come to Joshua Park.

COLBY

But I've told you, I'm not a very good organist!

EGGERSON

Don't say that, Mr. Simpkins, until you've tried our organ!

COLBY

Well, if you could induce them to try me ...

EGGERSON

The Parochial Church Council will be only too pleased,
And I have some influence. *I* am the Vicar's Warden.

COLBY

I'd like to apply.

EGGERSON

The stipend is small —
Very small, I'm afraid. Not enough to live on.
We'll have to think of other ways
Of making up an income. Piano lessons? —
As a temporary measure; because, Mr. Simpkins —
I hope you won't take this as an impertinence —
I don't see you spending a lifetime as an organist.
I think you'll come to find you've another vocation.
We worked together every day, you know,
For quite a little time, and I've watched you pretty closely.
Mr. Simpkins! You'll be thinking of reading for orders.
And you'll still have your music. Why, Mr. Simpkins,
Joshua Park may be only a stepping-stone
To a precentorship! And a canonry!

COLBY

We'll cross that bridge when we come to it, Eggers.
Oh, I'm sorry . . .

EGGERSON

Don't be sorry: I'm delighted.
And by the way, a practical point:
If you took the position, you'd want to find your feet
In Joshua Park, before you settled on lodgings;
We have a spare room. We should be most happy
If you cared to stop with us, until you were settled.

COLBY

I'd be very glad indeed — if Mrs. Eggerson approved.

EGGERSON

There'll be no one so pleased as Mrs. E.;
Of that I can assure you.

MRS. GUZZARD

        Mr. Eggerson,
I cannot see eye to eye with you,
Having been, myself, the wife of an organist;
But you too, I think, have had a wish realised.
— I believe that this interview can now be terminated.
If you will excuse me, Sir Claude . . .

SIR CLAUDE

                    Excuse you? Yes.

MRS. GUZZARD

I shall return to Teddington. Colby,
Will you get me a taxi to go to Waterloo?

COLBY

Get you a taxi? Yes, Aunt Sarah;
But I should see you home.

MRS. GUZZARD

        Home? Only to a taxi.
Do you mind if I take my leave, Sir Claude?
I'm no longer needed here.

                          [*Exit* COLBY]

SIR CLAUDE

        Mind? What do I mind?

MRS. GUZZARD

Then I will say goodbye. You have all had your wish
In one form or another. You and I, Sir Claude,
Had *our* wishes twenty-five years ago;
But we failed to observe, when we had our wishes,
That there was a time-limit clause in the contract.

SIR CLAUDE

What's that? Oh. Good bye, Mrs. Guzzard.

                    [*Exit* MRS. GUZZARD]

SIR CLAUDE

What's happened? Have they gone? Is Colby coming back?

LADY ELIZABETH

My poor Claude!
    [LUCASTA crosses to SIR CLAUDE and kneels beside him]

KAGHAN

You know, Claude, I think we all made the same mistake —
All except Eggers . . .

EGGERSON
Me, Mr. Kaghan?

KAGHAN

We wanted Colby to be something he wasn't.

LADY ELIZABETH

I suppose that's true of you and me, Claude.
Between not knowing what other people want of one,
And not knowing what one should ask of other people,
One does make mistakes! But I mean to do better.
Claude, we've got to try to understand our children.

KAGHAN

And we should like to understand *you* . . .
I mean, I'm including both of you,
Claude . . . and Aunt Elizabeth.
You know, Claude, both Lucasta and I
Would like to mean something to you . . . if you'd let us;
And we'd take the responsibility of meaning it.
        [LUCASTA *puts her arms around* SIR CLAUDE]

SIR CLAUDE

Don't leave me, Lucasta.
Eggerson! Do *you* really believe her?
            [EGGERSON *nods*]

CURTAIN

The Cast of the First Production
at the
Edinburgh Festival

August 25–September 5 1953

Sir Claude Mulhammer	PAUL ROGERS
Eggerson	ALAN WEBB
Colby Simpkins	DENHOLM ELLIOTT
B. Kaghan	PETER JONES
Lucasta Angel	MARGARET LEIGHTON
Lady Elizabeth Mulhammer	ISABEL JEANS
Mrs. Guzzard	ALISON LEGGATT

Presented by HENRY SHEREK

Directed by E. MARTIN BROWNE

Settings designed by HUTCHINSON SCOTT